NAEP
REPORTING PRACTICES

INVESTIGATING DISTRICT-LEVEL AND MARKET-BASKET REPORTING

Committee on NAEP Reporting Practices
Pasquale J. DeVito and Judith A. Koenig, *editors*

Center for Education
Board on Testing and Assessment

National Research Council

NATIONAL ACADEMY PRESS
Washington, D.C.

NATIONAL ACADEMY PRESS 2101 Constitution Avenue, N.W. Washington, DC 20418

NOTICE: The project that is the subject of this report was approved by the Governing Board of the National Research Council, whose members are drawn from the councils of the National Academy of Sciences, the National Academy of Engineering, and the Institute of Medicine. The members of the committee responsible for the report were chosen for their special competences and with regard for appropriate balance.

The study was supported by Contract/Grant No. EA 95083001 between the National Academy of Sciences and the Department of Education. Any opinions, findings, conclusions, or recommendations expressed in this publication are those of the author(s) and do not necessarily reflect the view of the organizations or agencies that provided support for this project.

Suggested citation: National Research Council. 2001. *NAEP Reporting Practices: Investigating District-Level and Market-Basket Reporting.* Committee on NAEP Reporting Practices. Pasquale J. DeVito and Judith A. Koenig, editors. Board on Testing and Assessment, Center for Education. Washington, DC: National Academy Press.

International Standard Book Number 0-309-07313-8

Additional copies of this report are available from National Academy Press, 2101 Constitution Avenue, N.W., Washington, DC 20418

Call (800) 624-6242 or (202) 334-3313 (in the Washington metropolitan area)

This report is also available online at **http://www.nap.edu**

Printed in the United States of America

THE NATIONAL ACADEMIES

National Academy of Sciences
National Academy of Engineering
Institute of Medicine
National Research Council

The **National Academy of Sciences** is a private, nonprofit, self-perpetuating society of distinguished scholars engaged in scientific and engineering research, dedicated to the furtherance of science and technology and to their use for the general welfare. Upon the authority of the charter granted to it by the Congress in 1863, the Academy has a mandate that requires it to advise the federal government on scientific and technical matters. Dr. Bruce M. Alberts is president of the National Academy of Sciences.

The **National Academy of Engineering** was established in 1964, under the charter of the National Academy of Sciences, as a parallel organization of outstanding engineers. It is autonomous in its administration and in the selection of its members, sharing with the National Academy of Sciences the responsibility for advising the federal government. The National Academy of Engineering also sponsors engineering programs aimed at meeting national needs, encourages education and research, and recognizes the superior achievements of engineers. Dr. William A. Wulf is president of the National Academy of Engineering.

The **Institute of Medicine** was established in 1970 by the National Academy of Sciences to secure the services of eminent members of appropriate professions in the examination of policy matters pertaining to the health of the public. The Institute acts under the responsibility given to the National Academy of Sciences by its congressional charter to be an adviser to the federal government and, upon its own initiative, to identify issues of medical care, research, and education. Dr. Kenneth I. Shine is president of the Institute of Medicine.

The **National Research Council** was organized by the National Academy of Sciences in 1916 to associate the broad community of science and technology with the Academy's purposes of furthering knowledge and advising the federal government. Functioning in accordance with general policies determined by the Academy, the Council has become the principal operating agency of both the National Academy of Sciences and the National Academy of Engineering in providing services to the government, the public, and the scientific and engineering communities. The Council is administered jointly by both Academies and the Institute of Medicine. Dr. Bruce M. Alberts and Dr. William A. Wulf are chairman and vice chairman, respectively, of the National Research Council.

COMMITTEE ON NAEP REPORTING PRACTICES: INVESTIGATING DISTRICT-LEVEL AND MARKET-BASKET REPORTING

PASQUALE DEVITO (*Chair*), Office of Assessment, Rhode Island Department of Education

LINDA BRYANT, Westwood Elementary School, Pittsburgh

C. MELODY CARSWELL, Department of Psychology, University of Kentucky

MARYELLEN DONAHUE, Office of Research, Assessment, and Evaluation, Boston Public Schools

LOU FABRIZIO, Division of Accountability Services, North Carolina Department of Public Instruction

LEANN GAMACHE, Assessment and Evaluation, Education Services Center, Littleton Public Schools, Littleton, Colorado

DOUGLAS HERRMANN, Department of Psychology, Indiana State University

AUDREY QUALLS, Iowa Testing Program, Iowa City, Iowa

MARK RECKASE, Department of Counseling, Educational Psychology, and Special Education, Michigan State University

DUANE STEFFEY, Department of Mathematical and Computer Sciences, San Diego State University

JUDITH KOENIG, *Study Director*
KAREN MITCHELL, *Senior Program Officer*
KAELI KNOWLES, *Program Officer*
DOROTHY MAJEWSKI, *Senior Project Assistant*

Acknowledgments

The Committee on NAEP Reporting Practices wishes to thank the many people who helped to make possible the preparation of this report. An important part of the committee's work was to gather information on the desirability, feasibility, and potential impact of district-level and market-basket reporting for the National Assessment of Education Progress (NAEP). Many people gave generously of their time during committee meetings and workshops and in preparing papers for the committee.

Staff from National Center for Education Statistics (NCES), under the direction of Gary Phillips, acting commissioner, and staff from the National Assessment Governing Board (NAGB), under the leadership of Roy Truby, executive director, were valuable sources of information. Peggy Carr, Patricia Dabbs, Arnold Goldstein, Steve Gorman, Andrew Kolstad, and Holly Spurlock of NCES and Roy Truby, Mary Lyn Bourque, Sharif Shakrani, Lawrence Feinberg, and Raymond Fields of NAGB provided the committee with important background information on numerous occasions. Papers prepared for the committee's workshops by Roy Truby and Andrew Kolstad were particularly helpful as were the papers and information provided by John Mazzeo and Robert Mislevy of ETS, and Keith Rust and Richard Valliant of Westat.

In September 1999, the committee held a workshop to gather information on issues related to district-level reporting for NAEP. A great many people contributed to the success of this workshop, which brought together representatives from state and local assessment offices, experts in educational measurement, and others familiar with the issues related to reporting district-level NAEP results. We are indebted to: Nancy Amuleru-Marshall, Atlanta Public Schools; Albert Beaton at Boston College's School of Education; Peter Behuniak, Connecticut State Department of Education; Carmen Chapman Pfeiffer, Illinois State Department of Education; Mitchell Chester, School District of Philadelphia; Judy Costa, Clark County School District in Nevada; Gerald DeMauro, Office of State Assessment in Albany, New York; Steve Dunbar with the University of Iowa's College of Education; Sharon Lewis, Council of the Great City Schools; Wayne Martin, Council of Chief State School Officers; Thomas McIntosh, Nevada Department of Education; Paula Mosley, Office of Instruction, Los Angeles; Carole Perlman, Chicago Public Schools; Edward Roeber, Measured Progress in Dover, New Hampshire; Harry Selig, Houston Independent School District; Robert Silverman, Office of Public Instruction in Olympia, Washington; Don Watson, Colorado Department of Education; and Lauress Wise, Human Resources Research Organization in Alexandria, Virginia.

The committee conducted a second workshop in February 2000 to collect information on issues related to market-basket reporting. We are grateful to the representatives from state and local assessment offices, experts in educational measurement, and others familiar with the issues related to market-basket reporting who helped make this workshop a success. The committee thanks the many panelists and discussants: R. Darrell Bock with University of Chicago's Departments of Psychology and Education; Paul Cieslak, Milwaukee Public Schools; Richard Lee Colvin, Los Angeles Times; Ronald Costello, Noblesville Schools in Indiana; Marlene Hartzman, Montgomery County Public Schools in Maryland; Paul Kimmelman with Illinois' West Northfield School District; David Kroeze with Illinois' Northbrook School District 27; Wayne Martin, Council of Chief State School Officers; Marilyn McConachie, Illinois State Board of Education; Donald McLaughlin, American Institutes for Research; Joseph O'Reilly, Mesa Unified School District in Arizona; Ken Stewart, Bureau of Labor Statistics; David Thissen, Department of Psychology, University of North Carolina, Chapel Hill; Carrol Thomas, Beaumont Independent School District in Texas; and C. Scott Trimble, Kentucky Department of Education. We are especially grateful to Patricia Kenney with the University of Michigan for her extensive review and discussion of the plans for constructing NAEP short forms.

We acknowledge the contribution of a number of individuals at the NRC who provided guidance and assistance at many stages during the organization of the workshops and the preparation of this report. We thank Michael Feuer, executive director of the Center for Education and former director of the Board on Testing and Assessment (BOTA), for his expert guidance and leadership of this project. We are indebted to BOTA staff officer, Karen Mitchell, for her assistance in planning both workshops and writing this report. Karen was a principal source of expertise in both the substance and process for this workshop. We also wish to thank BOTA staff members Patricia Morison, Alix Beatty, and Naomi Chudowsky for their assistance and advice during this study. We thank Kirsten Sampson Snyder for guiding the report through the review process and Yvonne Wise for her editorial assistance.

Special thanks are due to Dorothy Majewski, administrative associate, for her masterful handling of the logistical aspects of this project. In addition to handling the responsibilities associated with setting up committee meetings, Dorothy very capably managed the logistics of holding two workshops within a six-month period, each requiring arrangements for numerous panelists and guests. Subsequent to each workshop, a summary report was prepared and published, and Dorothy was of invaluable assistance in managing the logistics of manuscript preparation, distribution, and review.

Special thanks are also due to Kaeli Knowles, NRC program officer, for her fine work on this project. Kaeli played a major role in setting up the workshop on district-level reporting, contacting workshop participants and guiding them in developing their presentations. Kaeli's assistance during the preparation of both workshop summaries and this final report was immensely helpful.

This project could not have been completed without the capable leadership, management skills, and energy of Judith Koenig, study director. Judith skillfully guided the project through each of its phases to a successful completion. We, as a committee, are truly indebted to Judith for her superb work.

Above all, we thank the committee members for their outstanding contributions to this study. They drafted text, prepared background materials, and helped to organize and run workshops. During the course of the preparation of this final report, the committee chair assumed a new position as BOTA director. Committee members were superbly helpful during this transition, assisting with all aspects of report preparation including writing major portions of this report, responding to reviewer concerns, and revising text in accordance with reviewer comments. The chair is particularly grateful to his colleagues on the committee.

This report has been reviewed in draft form by individuals chosen for their diverse perspectives and technical expertise, in accordance with procedures approved by the NRC's Report Review Committee. The purpose of this independent review is to provide candid and critical comments that will assist the institution in making its published report as sound as possible and to ensure that the report meets institutional standards for objectivity, evidence, and responsiveness to the study charge. The review comments and draft manuscript remain confidential to protect the integrity of the deliberative process. We wish to thank the following individuals for their review of this report: Johnny Blair, University of Maryland, College Park; Chris Cross, Council for Basic Education, Washington, DC; Jonathan Dings, Boulder Valley Public Schools, Boulder, Colorado; Stephen Dunbar, University of Iowa; Paul Holland, Educational Testing Service, Princeton, New Jersey; Don McLaughlin, American Institutes for Research, Palo Alto, California; Thanos Patelis, The College Board, New York City.

Although the reviewers listed above have provided many constructive comments and suggestions, they were not asked to endorse the conclusions or recommendations nor did they see the final draft of the report before its release. The review of this report was overseen by Alan Schoenfeld, University of California, Berkeley, appointed by the Center for Education and Lyle Jones, University of North Carolina, Chapel Hill, appointed by the NRC's Report Review Committee, who were responsible for making certain that an independent examination of this report was carried out in accordance with institutional procedures and that all review comments were carefully considered. Responsibility for the final content of this report rests entirely with the authoring committee and the institution.

Pasquale J. DeVito
Chair

Contents

Executive Summary

Since 1969, the National Assessment of Educational Progress (NAEP) has been assessing educational attainment across the country. Mandated by Congress, NAEP surveys the educational accomplishments of students in the United States, monitors changes in achievement, and provides a measure of student learning at critical points in their school experience. NAEP results are summarized for the nation as a whole and for individual states with sufficient numbers of participating schools and students.

NAEP's sponsors believe that NAEP could provide useful data about educational achievement below the state level. They suggest that below state results "could provide an important source of data for informing a variety of education reform efforts at the local level" (National Assessment Governing Board, 1995b). In addition, district-level reporting could provide local educators with feedback in return for their participation in NAEP, something that NAEP's sponsors believe might increase motivation to participate in the assessment. Reporting results below the state level was prohibited until 1994. The Improving America's Schools Act of 1994, which reauthorized NAEP in that year, removed the language prohibiting below-state reporting and set the stage for consideration of reporting district-level and school-level results.

At the same time, NAEP's sponsors have been taking a critical look at their reporting procedures with an eye toward improving the usefulness and interpretability of reports. An overarching principle in their recent redesign policy is to define the audience for NAEP reports and to vary the kind and amount of detail in reports to make them most useful for the various audiences. Accordingly, NAEP's sponsors have funded studies to examine the ways in which reports are used by policy makers, educators, the press, and others and to identify common misuses and misinterpretations of reported data.

Within the context of the redesign proposals, the idea of market-basket reporting emerged as a way to better communicate what students in the United States know and are able to do at grade levels tested by NAEP. The market-basket concept is based on the idea that a relatively limited set of items can represent some larger construct. NAEP's sponsors draw parallels between the proposed NAEP market basket and the Consumer Price Index (CPI). The proposed NAEP market basket would consist of a publicly released collection of items intended to represent the content and skills assessed. Percent correct scores, a metric NAEP's sponsors believe is widely understood, will be used to summarize performance on the collection of items.

STUDY APPROACH

At the request of the Department of Education, the National Research Council formed the Committee on NAEP Reporting Practices to address questions about the desirability, feasibility, and potential impact of implementing these reporting practices. The committee developed study questions designed to address issues surrounding district-level and market-basket reporting. Study questions focused on the:

- characteristics and features of the reporting methods,
- information needs likely to be served,
- level of interest in the reporting practices,
- types of inferences that could be based on the reported data,
- implications of the reporting methods for NAEP, and
- implications of the reporting methods for state and local education programs.

To gather information on these issues, the committee reviewed the literature and policy statements on these two reporting practices; invited representatives from the National Assessment Governing Board (NAGB) and the National Center for Education Statistics (NCES) to attend their meetings and present information; attended NAGB board and subcommittee meetings; held a discussion during the Large Scale Assessment Conference sponsored by the Council of Chief State School Officers (CCSSO); arranged for a briefing on the CPI; and convened two multiday workshops. One workshop focused on district-level reporting, the other addressed market-basket reporting.

DISTRICT-LEVEL REPORTING

NAEP's sponsors believe that reporting district-level NAEP results would support local and state education reform efforts. Their rationale is that reporting NAEP performance for school districts has the potential to enable comparisons that cannot be made based on existing assessment results: comparisons of district-level achievement results across state boundaries and comparisons of district-level results with national assessment data.

Opinions about the desirability of such data are varied. Some participants in the committee's workshop believed the information would be uniquely informative. For example, comparisons among districts with similar demographic characteristics would allow them to identify those performing better than expected and instructional practices that work well. Others were attracted to the prospect of having a means for external validation and considered NAEP to be a stable external measure of achievement for making comparisons with their state and local assessment results. Another appealing feature to workshop participants was the possibility of assessment results in subject areas and grades not tested by their state or local programs. In addition, NAEP collects background data that many states and districts do not have the resources to collect, and they would look forward to receiving reports that associate district-level performance with background and school environmental data.

Other workshop participants were wary of the ways data might be used. Officials from some of the larger urban areas maintained that they were already aware that their children do not perform as well as those from other districts. Another set of assessment results would provide yet another opportunity for the press and others to criticize them. Some expressed concern about alignment issues, noting that their curricula do not necessarily match the material tested on NAEP. Attempts to use NAEP as a means of external validation for the state assessment would be problematic when the state assessment is aligned with instruction and NAEP is not, particularly if results from the different assessments suggest different findings about student achievement.

Given workshop participants' comments and the materials reviewed, the committee's most overriding concern about developing a program for reporting district-level NAEP results relates to districts' and states' levels of interest. Previous attempts at reporting district results (in 1996 and 1998) indicated virtually no interest in receiving district-level summaries of performance. Workshop participants' reactions were mixed, in part due to the lack of information about the goals, objectives, specifications, and costs of a district-level program. It is not clear what district-level reporting is intended to accomplish or whom the program would serve—only large urban districts or smaller districts as well. Decisions have not been made about the types of information districts and states would receive, when they would receive the information, how much it would cost, or who would pay the costs. These details need to be resolved before NAEP's sponsors can expect to gauge actual interest in receiving district-level results. Once the details are specified, then it is important to determine if there is sufficient interest to justify pursuing the program. On these points, the committee offers the following recommendations:

RECOMMENDATION: Market research emphasizing both needs analysis and product analysis is necessary to evaluate the level of interest in district-level reporting. The decision to move ahead with district-level reporting should be based on the results of market research conducted by an independent market-research organization. If market research suggests that there is little or no interest in district-level reporting, NAEP's sponsors should not continue to invest NAEP's limited resources pursuing district-level reporting.

RECOMMENDATION: If the decision is made to proceed with district-level reporting, NAEP's sponsors should develop and implement a plan for program evaluation, similar to the research conducted during the initial years of the Trial State Assessment, that would investigate the quality and utility of district-level NAEP data.

MARKET-BASKET REPORTING

Large-Scale Release of Items

The proposal for a NAEP market basket emanates from desires to make NAEP results more meaningful and more easily understood. According to workshop participants, the large-scale release of a market-basket set of items could demystify the assessment by providing many examples of the content and skills assessed and the format of items. Review of the content and skill coverage could stimulate discussions with local educators about their curricula and instructional programs. Review of NAEP item formats could lead to improvements in the design of items used with state, local, and classroom-based assessments. In addition, public review of the released materials could enhance understanding of the goals and purposes of the national assessment and might lead to increased public support for testing. Although workshop participants were generally positive about a large-scale release of items, they noted that a large release could be overly influential on local and state curricula or assessments. For instance, policy makers and educators concerned about their NAEP performance could attempt to align their curricula more closely with what is tested on NAEP. Assessment, curricula, and instructional practices form a tightly woven system—making changes to one aspect of the system can have an impact on other aspects of the system.

Percent Correct Scores

Using percent correct scores to summarize performance on the market basket is intended to make test results more user friendly. Because nearly everyone who has passed through the American school system has at one time or another been tested and received a percent correct score, most people could be expected to understand such scores. NAEP's sponsors believe that percent correct scores would have immediate meaning to the public.

Based on workshop participants' reactions, it is doubtful that percent correct scores would be more easily understood than the achievement-level results that NAEP currently reports. Many users have become accustomed to achievement level reporting; moving to a percent correct metric would require new interpretative assistance. Further, the use of this metric presents a number of challenges. For example, it is unclear whether percent correct scores would indicate percent of questions answered correctly or percent of possible points—both pose complications due to the mix of multiple-choice items and constructed response tasks scored on multipoint scales. In addition, NAEP results are not currently reported on a percent correct metric.

The NAEP Short Form

With the NAEP short form, the release of exemplar items would be smaller, but an intact form would be provided to states and districts to administer as they see fit. NAEP's sponsors hope that the short form will enable faster and more understandable reporting of results. Initial plans call for a fourth-grade mathematics short form, but the ultimate plan might be to develop short forms for a variety of subjects for states to use in years when NAEP assessments are not scheduled for particular subjects. The policy guiding development of the short forms stipulates that results be reported using NAEP achievement levels.

Many workshop participants found the idea of the short form to be appealing, but their comments reflected a variety of conceptions about the characteristics of a short form. Several envisioned the short form as a set of items that could be embedded into existing assessments to link results from state and local assessments with NAEP, while others viewed the short form as a mechanism for providing more timely reporting of NAEP results. Still others see it as a means for facilitating district-level or school-level reporting. It is not clear that all of these desired uses would be supported.

These widely divergent conceptions are exacerbated by the limited policy guidance NAGB has provided. While the generality of policy statements is appropriate so that developers are not limited in the approaches they might consider to put policy into practice, the lack of detail makes the short form an amorphous concept open to a variety of interpretations. Too many details remain undecided for the committee to make specific recommendations about the short form.

CONCLUSION: Thus far, the NAEP short form has been defined by general NAGB policy, but it has not been developed in sufficient technical and practical detail to allow potential users to react to a firm proposal. Instead, users are projecting into the general idea their own desired characteristics for the short form, such as an anchor for linking scales. Some of their

ideas and desires for the short form have already been determined to be problematic. It will not be possible for a short-form design to support all uses described by workshop participants.

Long Market Baskets versus Short-Form Market Baskets

All configurations for the market basket will involve tradeoffs. A market basket comprised of a large collection of items is more likely to be representative of the NAEP frameworks. As currently conceived, the NAEP short forms consist of approximately 30 items to be administered during a 60-minute testing period. A collection this small is unlikely to adequately represent the NAEP frameworks. Deriving results from the short form that are representative of the NAEP frameworks, technically sound, and comparable across versions of the short forms and to main NAEP results pose significant challenges. On these points, the committee makes the following recommendation.

> **RECOMMENDATION: All decisions about the configuration of the NAEP market basket will involve tradeoffs. Some methods for configuring the market basket would result in simpler procedures than others but would not support the desired inferences. Other methods would yield more generalizable results but at the expense of simplicity. If the decision is made to proceed with designing a NAEP market basket, its configuration should be based on a clear articulation of the purposes and objectives for the market basket.**

ANALOGIES WITH THE CONSUMER PRICE INDEX MARKET BASKET

Because analogies have frequently been made between the NAEP market basket and the Consumer Price Index (CPI), the committee investigated the extent to which such comparisons hold. In considering the proposals to develop and report a summary measure from the existing NAEP frameworks, the committee realized that the purpose and construction of the CPI market basket differs fundamentally from the corresponding elements of current NAEP proposals. The task of building an educational parallel to the CPI is formidable and appears to differ conceptually from the current NAEP market-basket development activities. Implementing a true "market-basket" approach in NAEP would thus necessitate major operational changes. Most importantly, a large national survey would need to be conducted to determine what students are actually taught in U.S. classrooms. Survey results would be used to construct the market basket, and then students would be tested to evaluate performance on the market basket.

Furthermore, the market-basket metaphor may be inappropriate. A market basket is an odd, even jarring image in the context of educational achievement. Most people do not see education as a consumer purchase or an assortment of independent parcels placed in a shopping cart. On these points, we find:

CONCLUSION: Use of the term "market basket" is misleading because (1) the NAEP frameworks reflect the aspirations of policy makers and educators and are not purely descriptive in nature and (2) the current operational features of NAEP differ fundamentally from the data collection processes used in producing the CPI.

RECOMMENDATION: In describing the various proposals for reporting a summary measure from the existing NAEP frameworks, NAEP's sponsors should refrain from using the term "market basket" because of inaccuracies in the implied analogy with the CPI.

RECOMMENDATION: If, given the issues raised about market-basket reporting, NAEP's sponsors wish to pursue the development of this concept, they should consider developing an educational index that possesses characteristics analogous to those of the Consumer Price Index: (1) is descriptive rather than reflecting policy makers' and educators' aspirations; (2) is reflective of regional differences in educational programs; and (3) is updated regularly to incorporate changes in curriculum.

ENHANCING REPORTS

When NAEP began reporting state-level results in 1990, researchers and others expressed concerns about potential misinterpretation or misuse of the data. Although not all the dire predictions came true, reports of below-state NAEP results increase the potential for misinterpretation problems. Given the amount of attention that below-state results would likely receive, whether derived from main NAEP or via a NAEP short form, significant attention should be devoted to product design.

As part of our study, the committee hoped to be able to review prototypic reports for the proposed reporting methods. While some preliminary examples of district-level and market-basket reports were available, NAEP's sponsors have not made definitive decisions about the format of reports. Given the stage of report design, we conducted a review of the literature on NAEP reporting procedures and examined examples of NAEP reports. Based on these reviews, we offer suggestions and recommendations for report design.

The design of data displays should be carefully evaluated and should evolve through methodical processes that consider the purposes of the data, the needs of users, the types of interpretations, and the anticipated types of misinterpretations. User-needs analysis is an appropriate forum for determining both product design and effective metaphors for aiding in communication.

Even if the proposals for district-level and market-basket reporting are not implemented, attention to the way NAEP information is provided would be useful. The types of NAEP reports are many and varied. The information serves many purposes for a broad constellation of audiences, including researchers, policy makers, the press, and the public. The more technical users as well as the lay public look to NAEP to support, refute, or inform their ideas about students' academic accomplishments. The messages taken from NAEP's data displays can easily influence their perceptions about the state of education in the United States. We therefore recommend:

RECOMMENDATION: Appropriate user profiles and needs assessments should be considered as part of the integrated design of district-level and market-basket reports. The integration of usability as part of the overall design process is essential because it considers the information needs of the public.

RECOMMENDATION: The text, graphs, and tables of reports developed for market-basket and district-level reporting should be subjected to standard usability engineering tech-

niques including appropriate usability testing methodologies. The purpose of such procedures would be to make reports more comprehensible to their readers and more accessible to their target audiences.

IMPLICATIONS FOR NAEP AND LOCAL EDUCATIONAL SYSTEMS

The two proposed reporting practices would provide new information that would receive attention from new audiences—audiences that may have not previously attended to NAEP results. The use of such information by policy makers, state and local departments of education, the press, and the lay public could have a significant impact on NAEP and on state and local assessment, curriculum, and instruction. In addition, these reporting methods pose challenges for NAEP's current procedures, including item development, sampling procedures, analytic and scoring methodologies, and report preparation.

NAEP has traditionally been a low-stakes assessment, but reporting results at a level closer to those responsible for instruction raises the stakes. With higher stakes comes the need to pay greater attention to security issues. In addition, motivation to do well may increase, which could affect the comparability of NAEP results across time and across jurisdictions, depending on how jurisdictions use the new results.

Introducing new products and procedures to an already complex system has significant cost and resource implications. To construct short forms and to accommodate security considerations, item development would need to be stepped up. Sampling procedures would need to be altered and additional students tested to support district-level results. Analytic methodologies would need to be adapted. The types and numbers of reports to be produced would affect report preparation, possibly increasing the length of time to release results. These factors would require fundamental changes in NAEP's processes, operations, and products.

For local education systems, the reporting practices could increase the attention on NAEP results. Current assessments might be replaced or altered to accommodate NAEP's schedule or to be modeled more closely after the NAEP frameworks and item formats. There could be efforts to align instructional programs more closely with the NAEP frameworks. If NAEP were to report percent correct scores, states and districts might consider following suit for local assessments and change to a metric that may not lead to improved understanding of NAEP or local test results. It is not clear that these changes would be beneficial to local education systems, and the implementation of these reporting approaches would require support systems to aid districts and states in appropriate uses and interpretations of the reported results. We therefore recommend:

RECOMMENDATION: The potential is high for significant impact on curriculum and /or assessment at the local levels. If either district-level reporting or market-basket reporting, with or without a short form, is planned for implementation, the program sponsors should develop and implement intensive support systems to assist districts and states in appropriate uses and interpretations of any such NAEP results reported.

1

Introduction

Since 1969, the National Assessment of Educational Progress (NAEP) has been assessing students across the country (U.S. Department of Education, 1999). Since its inception, NAEP has summarized academic performance for the nation as a whole and, beginning in 1990, for the individual states. Reporting results below the state level was prohibited until 1994. The Improving America's Schools Act of 1994, which reauthorized NAEP in that year, removed the language prohibiting below-state reporting and set the stage for consideration of reporting district-level and school-level results.

NAEP's policy-making body believes "below state results could provide an important source of data for informing a variety of education reform efforts at the local level" (National Assessment Governing Board, 1995a). Some districts have expressed interest in district-level NAEP with an eye toward augmenting their current assessments, filling in gaps for content areas not currently tested or even substituting NAEP instruments for those measures that have been locally developed or purchased (National Research Council, 1999c). NAEP's sponsors have also suggested district-level reports could increase motivation for districts' participation in the assessment by providing them with feedback on performance in return for their participation.

At the same time, NAEP's sponsors have taken a critical look at their reporting methods with the objective of improving the usefulness and interpretability of reports (National Assessment Governing Board, 1996; National Assessment Governing Board, 1999a). NAEP's sponsors have attempted over the years to produce reports of achievement results that were more usable by lay audiences and that contain more easily interpreted displays of the information. NAEP has experimented with a variety of approaches including, for example, reports that utilize a newspaper format, specific brochures of topical areas, and reports with easier-to-read graphs and tables (U.S. Department of Education, 1999). They have funded studies to examine the ways in which reports are used by policy makers, educators, the press, and others and to identify misuses and misinterpretations of reported data (Hambleton & Slater, 1996; Jaeger, 1995; Hambleton & Meara, 2000).

In addition, NAEP has attempted to design and introduce innovative research approaches to help with the interpretation of the data. Along this vein, advisers to the National Assessment Governing Board (NAGB) have proposed the use of "market-basket" reporting methods as another means to accomplish simpler reporting that may be more useful to NAEP's audiences (Forsyth, Hambleton, Linn, Mislevy, & Yen, 1996). Like the Consumer Price Index (CPI), which presents information on inflation by measuring price changes on a "market basket" of goods and services, a market-basket NAEP report would present information on student achievement based on a "market basket" of knowledge and skills in a content area. Under one scenario, for example, NAEP would report results as percentages of items correct on sets of representative items, an approach to reporting that could lead to easier-to-understand reports of student achievement. As part of their evaluation of NAEP, the National Research Council's Committee on the Evaluation of National and State Assessments of Educational Progress stressed the need for clear and comprehensible reporting metrics that would simplify the interpretation of results and encouraged exploration of market-basket reporting for NAEP (National Research Council, 1999b). Market-basket reporting might be expected to provide an easier-to-understand picture of students' academic accomplishments.

In pursuit of the goals of improved reporting and use of test results, NAEP's sponsors were interested in exploring the feasibility and potential impact of both district-level and market-basket reporting practices as well as the possible connections between them. Accordingly, at the request of the U.S. Department of Education, the National Research Council (NRC) established the Committee on NAEP Reporting Practices to study these reporting practices. Because these two topics are intertwined, the committee is examining them in tandem.

The committee developed two sets of study questions to address issues associated with district-level and market-basket reporting. With regard to district-level reporting, the committee examined the following:

1. What are the proposed characteristics of a district-level NAEP?
2. If implemented, what information needs might it serve?
3. What is the degree of interest in participating in district-level NAEP and what are the factors that would influence interest?
4. Would district-level NAEP pose any threats to the validity of inferences from national and state NAEP?
5. What are the implications of district-level reporting for other state and local assessment programs?

With respect to market-basket reporting, the committee investigated the following:

1. What is market-basket reporting?
2. How might reports of market-basket results be presented to NAEP's audiences? Are there prototypes?
3. What information needs might be served by market-basket reporting for NAEP?
4. Are market-basket results likely to be relevant and accurate enough to meet these needs?
5. Would market-basket reporting pose any threats to the validity of inferences from national and state NAEP? What types of inferences would be valid?
6. What are the implications of market-basket reporting for other national, state, and local assessment programs? What role might an NAEP short form play?

In addressing these issues, the committee considered the future context in which NAEP may be operating. For instance, the National Center for Education Statistics (NCES) set a priority to have all states sign up for NAEP and secured participation agreements with 48 states for the assessment in 2000. For numerous reasons, however, several states were unable to successfully take part in the assessment. In two states, one large district refused to participate, making it impossible for each of these states to meet participation criteria. Similarly, other states were unable to secure participation of enough schools to meet the threshold criteria. In fact, even some states that enacted legislation mandating state NAEP participation were unable to garner the necessary interest to meet the inclusion criteria (National Center for Education Statistics, 2000a).

Tied to the increasing difficulty in securing participation for NAEP is the proliferation of assessment programs in general. Because of state education reforms and the requirements of federal education legislation (e.g., Improving America's Schools Act (IASA), Individuals with Disabilities Education Act (IDEA), and Carl Perkins Act), state assessment programs have expanded greatly in both scope and complexity in the past decade (Council of Chief State School Officers, 2000). Similarly, many local school districts, particularly the large urban school districts so important to state NAEP sampling strategies, have expanded the use of assessment instruments in their own testing programs (National Research Council, 1999c).

Further, a potential factor in the changing context of NAEP is the proposal to make NAEP a more "high-stakes" measure by connecting rewards and/or sanctions to states' performance. For example, in its fiscal 2001 budget, the Clinton administration proposed a "Recognition and Reward Program" that would provide "high performance bonuses to states that make exemplary progress in improving student performance and closing the achievement gap between high- and low-performing groups of students" (National Center for Education Statistics, 2000b:2). While at the time of the writing of this report, it is impossible to predict if this proposal will be enacted, it remains a distinct possibility.

STUDY APPROACH

To gather information on the issues surrounding market-basket and district-level reporting, the committee reviewed the literature on these two topics, invited representatives from NAEP's sponsoring agencies (NAGB and NCES) to attend meetings and present information, attended NAGB board and subcommittee meetings, held a discussion during the Large-Scale Assessment Conference sponsored by the Council of Chief State School Officers (CCSSO), and conducted two multiday workshops specifically on these two topics. The workshops addressed key issues from a variety of perspectives. The purpose of the NRC's Workshop on District-Level Reporting for NAEP was to explore with various stakeholders their interest in and perceptions regarding the likely impacts of district-level reporting. Similarly, the purpose of the NRC's Workshop on Market-Basket Reporting was to explore with various stakeholders their interest in and perceptions regarding the desirability, feasibility, and potential impact of market-basket reporting for NAEP. Chapter 3 provides additional details about the workshop on district-level reporting; additional information about the workshop on market-basket reporting is included and Chapters 4 and 5.

WHAT IS DISTRICT-LEVEL REPORTING?

When first implemented, NAEP results were reported only for the nation as a whole. Following congressional authorization in 1988, the Trial State Assessment was initiated which allowed reporting of results for participating states, although below-state reporting was still prohibited. The 1994 reauthorization of NAEP removed this prohibition, but the law neither called for district or school-level reporting nor did it outline details about how such practices would operate. While NAGB and NCES have been exploring the issues associated with providing district-level results, the policies for district-level reporting are not yet in place nor are the details to guide program implementation.

WHAT IS MARKET-BASKET REPORTING?

Market-basket reporting was first discussed in connection with NAEP's redesign in 1996 (National Assessment Governing Board, 1996) and was again included in the most recent redesign effort, NAEP Design 2000-2010 (National Assessment Governing Board, 1999a). The market-basket concept is based on the idea that a limited set of items can represent some larger construct. The most common example of a market basket is the CPI, produced by the Bureau of Labor Statistics. The CPI tracks price changes paid by urban consumers in purchasing a locally representative set of consumer goods and services. The CPI measures monthly cost differentials for products in its market basket; therefore, the CPI is frequently used as an indicator of change in the U.S. economy. The CPI market-basket concept resonates with the general public; it invokes the tangible image of a shopper at the market filling a basket with a set of goods regarded as broadly reflecting consumer spending patterns at www.states.bls.gov (Bureau of Labor Statistics, 1999).

The general idea of a NAEP market basket draws on a similar image: a collection of test questions representative of some larger content domain; and an easily understood index to summarize performance on the items.

There are two components of the NAEP market basket: the collection of items and the summary index. The collection of items could be large (longer than a typical test form given to a student) or small (small enough to be considered an administrable test form). The summary index currently under consideration is the percent correct score (Mazzeo, 2000).

There are a number of configurations for a NAEP market basket. We discuss several in Chapter 4 of this report. To acquaint the reader with the basic ideas and issues associated with market-basket reporting, two alternative scenarios are portrayed in Figure 1-1.

Figure 1-1 presents a diagram of various components of the market basket and describes two alternate configurations. Under one scenario, a large collection of items would be assembled and released publicly. To adequately cover the breadth of the content domain, the collection would be much larger than any one of the forms used in the test and probably too long to administer to a single student at one sitting. This presents some challenges for the calculation of the percent correct scores. Because no student would take all of the items, complex statistical procedures would be needed for estimating scores. This alternative appears in Figure 1-1 as "scenario one."

A second scenario involves producing multiple "administrable" test forms (called "short forms"). Students would take an entire test form, and scores could be based on students' performance for the entire test in the manner usually employed by testing programs. Although this would simplify calculation of percent correct scores, the collection of items would be much smaller and less likely to adequately represent the content domain. This scenario also calls for assembling multiple test forms. Some forms would be released to the public, while others would remain secure, perhaps for use by state and local assessment programs, and possibly to be embedded into or administered in conjunction with existing tests. This alternative appears in Figure 1-1 as "scenario two."

ORGANIZATION OF THIS REPORT

This report begins with an overview of NAEP in Chapter 2. Chapter 3 is devoted to district-level reporting, and market-basket reporting is covered in Chapter 4. Because of the analogies that have been drawn between market-basket reporting and the CPI, we include discussion of the similarities and differences in Chapter 4; full details about construction and reporting of the CPI appear in Appendix A. The short form, which

FIGURE 1-1   Components of the NAEP Market Basket

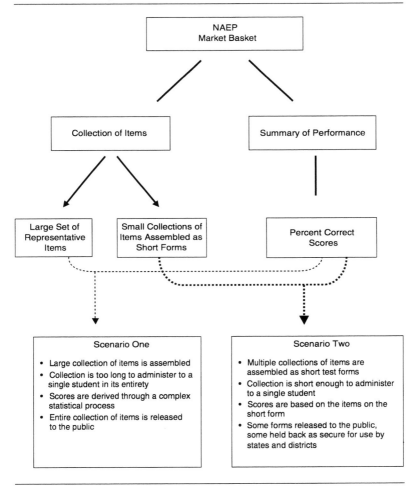

would be created under scenario two for the market basket, is addressed in Chapter 5. We believe that creation and administration of short-form NAEP would alter the fundamental purposes of NAEP, and we take up these issues of "changed NAEP" in this chapter.

NAEP's sponsors do not yet have prototypical models of either market-basket reports or district-level reports. During the course of our study, we reviewed a preliminary example of a market-basket report and a report provided to one district, but neither report was presented to us as a prototypic market-basket or district-level report. To get a better sense of the design and contents of such reports, we reviewed other current NAEP reports. In Chapter 6, we discuss ways NAEP's sponsors might formulate reports to ensure their usefulness, ease of understanding, and portrayal of meaningful information. A detailed example of an application of these procedures appears in Appendix B.

Both market-basket and district-level reporting could potentially affect the internal configuration of the NAEP program, because they pose challenges for sampling, scoring, and the number and types of reports to be prepared. For local school systems, reporting district-level results brings NAEP to a more intimate level of analysis. It is not too difficult to imagine district-level results included in accountability systems or put to other high-stakes uses, especially with the rewards that have been proposed (National Center for Education Statistics, 2000b). In Chapter 7, we present likely implications of the proposed reporting practices for NAEP and for local educational systems.

2

Current NAEP

This chapter begins with an overview of NAEP and highlights features of the current assessment program that bear on or may be affected by district-level and market-basket reporting practices. Later in the chapter, we address the issues and concerns about NAEP reports that prompted consideration of these two reporting methods.

OVERVIEW OF NAEP

As mandated by Congress in 1969, NAEP surveys the educational accomplishments of students in the United States. According to NAEP's sponsors, the program has two major goals: "to reflect current educational and assessment practices and to measure change reliably over time" (U.S. Department of Education, 1999:3). The assessment informs national- and state-level policy makers about student performances, and thus plays an integral role in evaluations of the conditions and progress of the nation's educational system.

In addition, NAEP has proven to be a unique source of background information that has both informed and guided educational policy. Currently, NAEP includes two distinct assessment programs with different instrumentation, sampling, administration, and reporting practices, referred to as *long-term trend* NAEP and *main* NAEP (U.S. Department of Education, 1999).

Components of NAEP

Long-term trend NAEP is a collection of test items in reading, writing, mathematics, and science that have been administered many times over the last three decades. As the name implies, trend NAEP is designed to document changes in academic performance over time. During the past decade, trend NAEP was administered in 1990, 1992, 1994, 1996, and 1999. Trend NAEP is administered to nationally representative samples of 9-, 13-, and 17-year olds (U.S. Department of Education, 1999).

Main NAEP test items reflect current thinking about what students know and can do in the NAEP subject areas. They are based on recently developed content and skill outlines in reading, writing, mathematics, science, U.S. history, world history, geography, civics, the arts, and foreign languages. Main NAEP assessments use the latest advances in assessment methodology. Typically, two subjects are tested at each biennial administration. Main NAEP has two components: national NAEP and state NAEP.

National NAEP tests nationally representative samples of students in grades four, eight, and twelve. In most subjects, NAEP is administered two, three, or four times during a 12-year period, making it possible to track changes in performance over time.

State NAEP assessments are administered to representative samples of students in states that elect to participate. State NAEP uses the same large-scale assessment materials as national NAEP. It is administered to grades four and eight in reading, writing, mathematics, and science (although not always in both grades in each of these subjects).

ANALYTIC PROCEDURES

NAEP differs fundamentally from other testing programs in that its objective is to obtain accurate measures of academic achievement for groups of students rather than for individuals. This goal is achieved using innovative sampling, scaling, and analytic procedures.

Sampling of Students

NAEP tests a relatively small proportion of the student population of interest using probability sampling methods. The national samples for main NAEP are selected using stratified multistage sampling designs with three stages of selection: districts, schools, and students. The result is a sample of about 150,000 students sampled from 2,000 schools. The sampling design for state NAEP has only two stages of selection: schools and students within schools and samples approximately 3,000 students in 100 schools per state (roughly 100,000 students in 4,000 schools nationwide). The school and student sampling plan for trend NAEP is similar to the design for national NAEP. In 1996, between 3,500 and 5,500 students were tested in mathematics and science and between 4,500 and 5,500 were tested in reading and writing (Campbell, Voekl, & Donahue, 1997).

Sampling of Items

NAEP assesses a cross section of the content within a subject-matter area. Due to the large number of content areas and sub-areas within those content areas, NAEP uses a matrix sampling design to assess students in each subject. Using this design, blocks of items drawn from each content domain are administered to groups of students, thereby making it possible to administer a large number and range of items while keeping individual testing time to one hour for all subjects. Consequently, students receive different but overlapping sets of NAEP items using a form of matrix sub-sampling known as *balanced incomplete block spiraling*. This design requires highly complicated analyses and does not permit the performance of a particular student to be accurately measured. Therefore, NAEP reports only group-level results, and individual results are not provided.

Analytic Procedures

Although individual results are not reported, it is possible to compute estimates of individuals' performance on the overall assessment using complex statistical procedures. The observed data reflect student performance over the particular NAEP block the student actually took. Given that no individual takes all NAEP blocks, statistical estimation procedures must be used to derive estimates of individuals' proficiency on the full complement of skills and content covered by the assessment. The procedure involves combining samples of values drawn from distributions of possible proficiency estimates for each student. These individual student distributions are estimated from their responses to the test items and from background variables. The use of background variables in estimating proficiency is called *conditioning*.

For each student, five values, called *plausible values*, are randomly drawn from the student's distribution of possible proficiency estimates. Five plausible values are drawn to reflect the uncertainty in a student's proficiency estimate, given the limited set of test questions administered to each student. The sampling from the student's distribution is an application of Rubin's (1987) multiple imputation method for handling missing data (the responses to items not presented to the student are considered missing). In the NAEP context this process is called *plausible values methodology* (National Research Council, 1999b).

The conditioning process derives performance distributions for each student using information about performance of other students with similar background characteristics. That is, performance estimates are based on the assumption that a student's performance is likely to be similar to that of other students with similar backgrounds. Conditioning is performed differently for national and state NAEP. For national NAEP, it is based on the relationship between background variables and performance on test items for the national sample. For state NAEP, conditioning is based on the relationship between the background variables and item performance for each state; these relationships may not be the same for the different state samples. As a result, the estimated distributions of proficiency for two individuals with similar background characteristics and item responses may differ if the individuals are from different states.

REPORTING NAEP RESULTS

Statistics Reported

NAEP's current practice is to report student performance on the assessments using a scale that ranges from 0 to 500. Scale scores summarize performance in a given subject area for the nation as a whole, for individual states, and for subsets of the population based on demographic and background characteristics. Results are tabulated over time to provide trend information.

In addition, NAEP reports performance using performance standards, or achievement levels. The percentage of students at or above each achievement level is reported. NAGB has established, by policy, definitions for three levels of student achievement: basic, proficient, and advanced (U.S. Department of Education, 1999). The achievement levels describe the range of performance NAGB believes should be demonstrated at each grade. NAGB's definitions for each level are as follows (U.S. Department of Education, 1999:29):

- *Basic:* partial mastery of prerequisite knowledge and skills that are fundamental for proficient work at each grade.
- *Proficient:* solid academic performance for each grade assessed. Students reaching this level have demonstrated competency over challenging subject matter, including subject-matter knowledge, application of such knowledge to real-world situations, and analytical skills appropriate to the subject matter.
- *Advanced:* superior performance

NAEP also collects a variety of demographic, background, and contextual information on students, teachers, and administrators. Student demographic information includes characteristics such as race/ethnicity, gender, and highest level of parental education. Contextual and environmental data provide information about students' course selection, homework habits, use of textbooks and computers, and communication with parents about schoolwork. Information obtained about teachers includes the training they received, the number of years they have taught, and the instructional practices they employ. Administrators also respond to questions about their schools, including the location and type of school, school enrollment numbers, and levels of parental involvement. NAEP summarizes achievement results by these various characteristics.

Types of Reports

NAEP produces a variety of reports, each targeted to a specific audience. According to NCES, targeting each report to a segment of the audience increases its impact and appeal (U.S. Department of Education, 1999). Table 2-1 below lists the various types of NAEP reports along with the targeted audience and general purpose for each type of report.

Uses of NAEP Reports

The Committee on the Evaluation of National and State Assessments of Educational Progress conducted an analysis of the uses of the 1996 NAEP mathematics and science results. The analysis considered reports of NAEP results in the popular and professional press, NAEP publications, and vari-

TABLE 2-1

Type of Report	Targeted Audience	Purpose/Contents
NAEP Report Cards	Policy makers	Present results for all test takers and for various population groups
Highlights Reports	Parents, school board members, general public	Answer frequently asked questions in non-technical manner
Instructional Reports	Educators, school administrators, and subject-matter experts	Include many of the educational and instructional material available from the NAEP assessments.
State Reports	Policy makers, Department of Education officials, chief state school officers	Present results for all test takers and various population groups for each state.
Cross-State Data Compendia	Researchers and state testing directors	Serve as reference documents that accompany other reports and present state-by-state results for variables included in the state reports.
Trend Reports	[Not specified]	Describe patterns and changes in student achievement as measured by the long-term trend assessments.
Focused Reports	Educators, policy makers, psychometricians, and interested citizens	Explore in-depth questions with broad educational implications.
Summary Data Tables	[Not specified]	Present extensive tabular summaries based on background data from student, teacher, and school questionnaires.
Technical Reports	Educational researchers, psychometricians, and other technical audiences	Document details of the assessment, including sample design, instrument development, data collection process, and analytic procedures.

ous letters, memoranda, and other unpublished documents. They found that NAEP results were used to (National Research Council, 1999b:27):

1. describe the status of the educational system,
2. describe student performance by demographic group,
3. identify the knowledge and skills over which students have (or do not have) mastery,
4. support judgments about the adequacy of observed performance,
5. argue the success or failure of instructional content and strategies,
6. discuss relationships among achievement and school and family variables,
7. reinforce the call for high academic standards and educational reform, and
8. argue for system and school accountability.

These findings are similar to those cited by McDonnell (1994).

Redesigning NAEP Reports

The diverse audiences and uses for NAEP reports have long posed challenges for the assessment (e.g., Koretz and Deibert, 1995/1996). Concern about appropriate uses and potential misinterpretations were heightened by the media's reporting on the results of the first Trial State Assessment (Jaeger, 1998). One of the most widespread interpretation problems was the media translation of mean NAEP scores into state rankings. Many newspapers simply ranked states according to average scores, notwithstanding the fact that differences among state scores were not statistically reliable.

In addition, there have been misinterpretations associated with reporting of achievement-level results. The method of reporting the percentage of students at or above each achievement level has been found to cause confusion (Hambleton & Slater, 1995). Because the proportion of students at or above the advanced level are also above the basic and proficient levels, and the proportion at or above proficient are also above basic, the percentages of students at or above all three levels add up to more than 100 percent. This is confusing to users. The mental arithmetic that is required to determine the percentage that scored at a specific achievement level is difficult for many users of NAEP data. Other studies have cited difficulties associated with interpreting standard errors, significance levels, and other statistical jargon included in NAEP reports (Jaeger, 1996; Hambleton & Slater, 1995).

NAEP's sponsors have sought ways to improve its reports. The 1996 redesign of NAEP described the concept of market-basket reporting as one means for making reports more meaningful and understandable (National Assessment Governing Board, 1996). The authors of the document reasoned that public release of the market basket of items would give users a concrete reference for the meaning of the scores. This method would also have the advantage of being more comfortable to users who are "familiar with only traditional test scores," such as those reported as percents correct (Forsyth et al, 1996:6-26).

The most recent design plan, Design 2000-2010 (National Assessment Government Board, 1999a), again addressed reporting issues. Authors of the document set forth the objective of defining the audience for NAEP reports. They distinguished among NAEP's audiences by pointing out that the primary *audience* is the U.S. public, while the primary *users* of its data have been national and state policy makers, educators, and researchers. The document stated (National Assessment Governing Board, 1999a:10):

> [NAEP reports] should be written for the American public as the primary audience and should be understandable, free of jargon, easy to use and widely disseminated. National Assessment reports should be of high technical quality, with no erosion of reliability, validity, or accuracy.

> The amount of detail in reporting should be varied. *Comprehensive reports* would be prepared to provide an in-depth look at a subject, using new adopted test framework, many students, many test questions, and ample background information. Results would be reported using achievement levels. Data also would be reported by sex, race-ethnicity, socio-economic status (SES), and for public and private schools. *Standard reports* would provide overall results in a subject with achievement levels and average scores. Data could be reported by sex, race/ethnicity, SES, and for public and private schools, but would not be broken down further. *Special, focused assessments* on timely topics also would be conducted, exploring a particular question or issue and possible limited to one or two grades.

SUMMARY AND RECOMMENDATIONS

NAEP serves a diverse audience with varied interests and needs. Communicating assessment results to such a broad audience presents unique challenges. The breadth of the audiences combined with their differing needs and uses for the data make effective communication particularly difficult. The Committee on NAEP Reporting Practices views market-basket and district-level reporting as falling within the context of making NAEP results more useful and meaningful to a variety of audiences. These are important goals that deserve focused attention.

RECOMMENDATION 2-1: We support the efforts thus far on the design of NAEP reports and encourage NAEP's sponsors to continue to find ways to report NAEP results in ways that engage the public and enhance their understanding of student achievement in the United States.

3

Reporting District-Level NAEP Results

The Improving America's Schools Act of 1994, which reauthorized NAEP in that year, eliminated the prohibition against reporting NAEP results below the state level. Although the law removed the prohibition, it neither called for district- or school-level reporting, nor did it outline details about how such practices would operate. NAGB and NCES have explored reporting district-level results as a mechanism for providing more useful and meaningful NAEP data to local policy makers and educators. They have twice experimented with trial district-level reporting programs. For a variety of reasons, neither attempt revealed much interest on the part of school districts. The lack of interest was attributable, in part, to financial considerations and to unclear policy about whether the state or the district had the ultimate authority to make participation decisions. Despite the apparent lack of interest during the attempted trial programs, there is some evidence that provision of district-level results could be a key incentive to increasing schools' and districts' motivation to participate in NAEP (Ambach, 2000).

The focus of the committee's work on district-level reporting was to evaluate the desirability, feasibility, potential uses, and likely impacts of providing district-level NAEP results. In this chapter, we address the following questions: (1) What are the proposed characteristics of a district-level NAEP? (2) If implemented, what information needs might it serve? (3) What is the degree of interest in participating in district-level NAEP? (4) What factors would influence interest?

STUDY APPROACH

To gather information relevant to these questions, the committee reviewed the literature that has been written about below-state reporting, including NCES and NAGB policy guidelines for district-level reporting (National Assessment Governing Board, 1995a; National Assessment Governing Board, 1995b; National Center for Education Statistics, 1995); listened to presentations by representatives from NAGB, NCES, and their contractors (ETS and Westat) regarding district-level reporting; and held a workshop on district-level reporting. During the workshop, representatives of NAGB and NCES discussed policy guidelines, prior experiences, and future plans for providing district-level data. Representatives from ETS and Westat spoke about the technical issues associated with reporting district-level data. Individuals representing state and district assessment offices participated and commented on their interest in and potential uses for district-level results. Representatives from national organizations (Council of Chief State School Officers and Council of Great City Schools) and authors of papers on providing below-state NAEP results served as discussants at the workshop. Approximately 40 individuals participated in the workshop. Workshop proceedings were summarized and published (National Research Council, 1999c).

This chapter begins with a review of the concerns expressed when state NAEP was first implemented, as they could all relate to below-state reporting. This section contains a description of the evaluations of the Trial State Assessment, the findings of the evaluations, and the reported benefits of state NAEP. The chapter continues with a summary of the chief issues raised by authors who have explored the advantages and disadvantages of providing below-state results. In the next portion of this chapter, the two experiences with district-level reporting are described. The first of these experiences is associated with the 1996 assessment, and the other is associated with the 1998 assessment. A summary of the information obtained during the committee's workshop on district-level reporting is presented in the final portion of this chapter.

INITIAL CONCERNS FOR STATE-LEVEL REPORTING

Prior to implementation of the Trial State Assessment (TSA) and reporting of state-level results, researchers and others familiar with NAEP expressed concerns about the expansion of the assessment to include state-level data. These concerns centered around the anticipated uses of state-level data and the likely effects on curriculum and instruction. National NAEP had been a low-stakes examination, since data could not be used for decisions at the state, district, school, or classroom level. National-level data were not being used for accountability purposes, and participants were relatively unaffected by the results. With the provision of state-level results, some expressed concern that the stakes associated with NAEP could rise.

Specifically, observers questioned if the reporting of the TSA would cause local districts and states to change the curriculum or instruction that is provided to students. They also questioned if local or state testing programs would change to accommodate NAEP-tested skills or would simply be pushed aside. Observers also debated whether any changes in curriculum or assessment would be positive or counterproductive (Stancavage, Roeber, & Bohrnstedt, 1992:261).

These questions stemmed from concerns about the emphases given NAEP results. As long as NAEP was a low-stakes test and decisions did not rest on the results, it was unlikely that states and districts would adjust their curriculum or assessments based on the results. But reporting results at the state level could increase pressure on states to change their instructional practices, which could threaten the validity of NAEP scores (Koretz 1991:21). Furthermore, Koretz warned that changes in instructional practices could harm student learning. To the degree that NAEP frameworks represent the full domain of material students should know, planning instruction around the frameworks may be appropriate. However, if schools "teach to the test," meaning that they teach only a narrow domain covered by the assessment, then they have inappropriately narrowed the curriculum.

Beaton (1992:14) used the term "boosterism" to describe the activities that might be used to motivate students to do their best for the "state's honor." He suggested that boosterism combined with teaching to the test and "more or less subtle ways of producing higher scores" could affect the comparability of state trend data, if these practices change or become more effective over time.

Others questioned how the results might be interpreted. For instance, Haertel (1991:436) pointed out that the first sorts of questions asked will pertain to which states have the best educational systems but cautioned that attempts to answer would be "fraught with perils." Haertel continued (p.437):

[Comparisons] will involve generalizations from TSA exercise pools to a broader range of learning outcomes . . . [Such comparisons] depend on the match between NAEP content and states' own curriculum framework . . . For example, a state pressing to implement the [National Council of Teachers of Mathematics] framework might experience a (possibly temporary) decrease in performance on conventional mathematics problems due to its deliberate decision to allocate decreased instruction time to that type of problem. The 1990 TSA might support the (valid) inference that the state's performance on that type of problem was lagging, but not the (invalid) inference that their overall mathematics performance was lagging.

Haertel (1991) also expected that state-to-state comparisons would prompt the press and others to rank states, based on small (even trivial) differences in performance. In fact, Stancavage et al. (1992) reported that in spite of cautions by NCES and Secretary of Education Lamar Alexander not to rank states, four of the most influential newspapers in the nation did so. In a review of 55 articles published in the top 50 newspapers, they found that state rankings were mentioned in about two-thirds of the articles (Stancavage et al., 1992).

Other concerns pertained to the types of inferences that NAEP's various audiences might draw based on the background, environmental, and contextual data that are reported. These data provide a wealth of information on factors that relate to student achievement. However, the data collection design does not support inferences that these factors caused the level of achievement students attained nor does it meet the needs of accountability purposes. The design is cross sectional in nature, assessing different samples of students on each testing occasion. Such a design does not allow for the before-and-after data required to hold educators responsible for results. Furthermore, correlations of student achievement on NAEP with data about instructional practices obtained from the background information do not imply causal relationships. For example, the 1994 NAEP reading results showed that fourth-grade students who received more than 90 minutes of reading instruction a day actually performed worse than students receiving less instruction. Clearly, the low-performing students received more hours of instruction as a result of their deficiencies; the extra instruction did not cause the deficiencies (Glaser, Linn, & Bohrnstedt, 1997).

Benefits Associated with State NAEP

Despite these concerns about the provision of state-level data, reviews of the TSA have cited numerous benefits and positive impacts of the program. Feedback from state assessment officials indicated that state NAEP has had positive influences on instruction and assessment (Stancavage et al., 1992; Stancavage, Roeber, & Bohrnstedt, 1993; Hartka & Stancavage, 1994; DeVito, 1997). When the TSA was first implemented, many states were in the process of revamping their frameworks and assessments in both reading and mathematics. According to state officials, in states where changes were under way, the TSA served to validate the changes being implemented; in states contemplating changes, the TSA served as an impetus for change.

Respondents to surveys conducted by Stancavage and colleagues (Hartka & Stancavage, 1994) reported that the following changes in reading assessment and instruction were taking place: increased emphasis on higher-order thinking skills; better alignment with current research on reading; development of standards-based curricula; increased emphasis on literature; and better integration or alignment of assessment and instruction. Although these changes could not be directly attributed to the implementation of the TSA, they reflected priorities also set for the NAEP reading assessment. In addition, many state assessment measures were expanded to include more open-ended response items, with an increased emphasis on the use of authentic texts and passages, like those found on NAEP (Hartka & Stancavage, 1994).

At the time of the first TSA, the new mathematics standards published by the National Council of Teachers of Mathematics (NCTM) were having profound effects on mathematics curricula, instructional practice, and assessment throughout the country (Hartka & Stancavage, 1994). Survey results indicated that changes similar to those seen for reading were occurring in mathematics instruction and assessment: alignment with the NCTM standards, increased emphasis on higher-order thinking skills and problem solving, development of standards-based curricula, and integration or alignment of assessment and instruction (Hartka & Stancavage, 1994). The mathematics TSA was also influential in "tipping the balance in favor of calculators (in the classroom and on assessments) and using sample items [for] teacher in-service training" (Hartka & Stancavage, 1994:431). Again, although these changes could not be attributed to the TSA, the NAEP mathematics frameworks' alignment with the NCTM standards served to reinforce the value of the professional standards.

In 1990, results from the first TSA in 1990 garnered much attention from the media and the general public. For states with unsatisfactory performance, TSA results were helpful in spurring reform efforts. For states with satisfactory TSA performance, state officials could attribute the results to the recent reforms in their instructional practice and assessment measures.

LITERATURE ON BELOW- STATE REPORTING

In "The Case for District- and School-Level Results from NAEP," Selden (1991) made the seemingly self-evident argument that having information is better than not having it, saying (pg. 348), "most of the time, information is useful, and the more of it we have, the better, as long as the information is organized and presented in a way that [makes] it useful." Selden claimed that because NAEP is conducted and administered similarly across sites (schools), it offers comparable information from site to site, thus allowing state-to-state or district-to-district comparisons. He finds that NAEP's ability to collect high quality data comparably over time and across sites lends it to powerful uses for tracking both student achievement and background information. According to Selden, questions that might be addressed by trend data include: are instructional practices changing in the desired directions; are the characteristics of the teacher workforce getting better; and are home reading practices improving. He explained that schools and districts could use trend information to examine their students' achievement in relation to instructional methods.

While Selden presented arguments in favor of providing below-state-level results, he and others (Haney and Madaus, 1991; Beaton, 1992; Roeber, 1994) also cautioned that reporting results below the state level could lead to a host of problems and misuses. Their arguments emphasized that, although having more information could be viewed as better than having less information, it is naïve to ignore the uses that might be made of the data. Indeed, Selden (1991:348) pointed out that one fear is that new information will be "misinterpreted, misused, or that unfortunate, unforeseen behavior will result from it." Reports of below-state NAEP results could easily become subject to inappropriate high-stakes uses. For example, results could be used for putting districts or schools into receivership; making interdistrict and interschool comparisons; using results in school choice plans; holding teachers accountable; and allocating resources on the basis of results (Haney and Madaus, 1991). In addition, some authors worried that NAEP's use as a high-stakes accountability device at the local level could lead to teaching to the test and distortion of the curriculum (Selden,

1991, Beaton, 1992). Selden (1991) further argued that the use of NAEP results at the district or school level has the potential to discourage states and districts from being innovative in developing their own assessments.

Potential high-stakes uses of NAEP would heighten the need for security. Item development would need to be stepped up, which would raise costs (Selden, 1991). NAGB, NCES, the NAEP contractors, and participating school district staff, would also have to coordinate efforts to ensure that the NAEP assessments are administered in an appropriate manner. According to Roeber (1994:42), such overt action would be needed "to assure that reporting does not distort instruction nor negatively impact the validity of the NAEP results now reported at the state and national levels."

EXPERIENCES WITH DISTRICT-LEVEL REPORTING

NAGB and NCES supported the initiative to provide district-level results, hoping that school districts would choose to use NAEP data to inform a variety of education reform initiatives at the local level (National Assessment Governing Board, 1995a; National Assessment Governing Board, 1995b). With the lifting of the prohibition against below-state reporting, NAGB and NCES explored two different procedures for offering district-level NAEP data to districts and states: the Trial District Assessment, offered in 1996, and the Naturally-Occurring District Plan, offered in 1998.

The 1996 Experience: Trial District Assessment

Under the Trial District Assessment, large school districts were offered three options for participating in district-level reporting of NAEP (National Center for Educational Statistics, 1995). The first option, "Augmentation of State NAEP Assessment," offered district-level results in the same subjects and grades as in state NAEP by augmenting the district's portion of the state NAEP sample. Under this option, districts would add "a few schools and students" to their already selected sample in order to report stable estimates of performance at the district level. According to the NCES, the procedures for augmenting the sample would "minimize the cost of the assessment process," and costs were to be paid by the district.

The second option in 1996, "Augmentation of National Assessment," would allow for reporting district results in subjects and grades administered as part of national NAEP by augmenting the number of schools selected within certain districts as part of the national sample. Because few schools are selected in any single district for national NAEP, this second option would require most school districts to select "full samples of schools" (National Center for Education Statistics, 1995:2) to meet the sampling requirements and to report meaningful results. The cost for augmenting the national sample for participating districts would be more substantial than those associated with augmenting the state sample. If a district selected either of these options, the procedures for sample selection, administration, scoring, analysis, and reporting would follow those established for national or state NAEP, depending on the option selected. And the results would be "NAEP comparable or equivalent."

The third option in 1996, "Research and Development," was offered to districts that might not desire NAEP-comparable or equivalent results but that had alternative ideas for using NAEP items. For example, districts might assess a subject or subjects not assessed by NAEP at the national or state level; they might want to administer only a portion of the NAEP instrument; or they might choose to deviate from standard NAEP procedures. NCES would regard such uses as research and development activities and would not certify the results obtained under this option as NAEP comparable or equivalent.

Prior to the 1996 administrations, NCES (with the assistance of the sampling contractor, Westat) determined that the minimum sampling requirements for analysis and reporting at the district level were 25 schools and 500 assessed students per grade and subject. To gauge interest in the plan, NCES and ETS sponsored a meeting during the 1995 annual meeting of the American Educational Research Association, inviting representatives from several of the larger districts in the country. Based on this meeting and further interaction with district representatives, NCES identified approximately 10 school systems interested in obtaining their NAEP results. NCES and their contractors held discussions with representatives of these districts. The costs turned out to be much higher than school systems could easily absorb (National Research Council, 1999c). Consequently, only Milwaukee participated in 1996, with financial assistance from the National Science Foundation. Additional sampling of schools and students was required for Milwaukee to reach the minimum numbers necessary for participation, and they received results only for grade eight.

Milwaukee's Experience under the Trial District Assessment

In the spring of 1996, NAEP was administered to a sample of Milwaukee's school population, and results were received in September 1997. NCES prepared a special report for the school district summarizing performance overall and by demographic, environmental, background, and academic characteristics. Explanatory text accompanied the tabular reports.

Paul Cieslak, former research specialist with the Milwaukee school district, attended the committee's workshop and described the uses made of the reported data. According to Cieslak, the report was primarily used as part of a day-long training session with 45 math/science resource teachers, under the district's NSF Urban Systemic Mathematics/Science Initiative to help the teachers work with project schools (Cieslak, 2000). The teachers found the overall performance and demographic information moderately helpful. The reports summarizing performance by teaching practices and by background variables and institutional practices were more useful and interesting. Milwaukee officials found that the NAEP results generally supported the types of instructional practices they had been encouraging.

According to Cieslak (2000), the School Environmental data "increased the value of the NAEP reports tenfold" since districts do not have the time or the resources to collect these data. This information helped school officials to look at relationships among classroom variables and performance. Cieslak believed that availability of the School Environmental data could be one of the strongest motivating factors behind districts' interest in participation.

While no specific decisions were based on the data, Cieslak believed that was primarily because so much attention is focused on their state and local assessments, especially those included in the district's accountability plan. In Milwaukee, the various assessment programs compete for attention, and the statewide assessments usually win out. Cieslak believes that state assessments will continue to receive most of the attention unless some strategies are implemented to demonstrate specifically how NAEP data are related to national standards, specific math/science concepts, or district goals.

The 1998 Experience: Naturally Occurring Districts

Prior to the 1998 NAEP administration, NCES and Westat determined that there were six "naturally occurring districts" in state samples.

They defined naturally occurring districts as those that comprise at least 20 percent of the state's sample and that meet the minimum sampling requirements for analysis and reporting at the district level (25 schools and 500 assessed students per grade and subject). These districts can be thought of as "self-representing in state NAEP samples" (Rust, 1999). The districts that met these guidelines in 1998 were Albuquerque, New Mexico; Anchorage, Alaska; Chicago, Illinois; Christiana County, Delaware; Clark County, Nevada; and New York City, New York.

In July 1998, NCES contacted district representatives to assess their interest in receiving district-level NAEP results at no additional cost. They found no takers. Alaska did not participate in 1998, and Christiana County expressed no interest. District representatives in New York City and Chicago did not want the data. Gradually, the idea of providing district-level reports grew increasingly controversial. The NAEP State Network, which consists of state assessment directors or their appointed representatives, voiced concerns about the fairness of making the data available for some districts but not others. NCES did not query Clark County or Albuquerque, or their respective states, as to their interest, since by then the idea of district-level reporting was being questioned (Arnold Goldstein, National Center for Education Statistics, personal communication, October 1999).

Controversy arose concerning who would make participation and release decisions for a district-level NAEP. Although New York and Chicago did not want the data, their respective states did, thereby creating a conflict. NAGB discussed the issue at its August 1999 meeting and decided that no further offers of district results should be made until it was clear who should be the deciding entity (National Assessment Governing Board, 1999d).

TECHNICAL AND POLICY CONSIDERATIONS FOR DISTRICT-LEVEL REPORTING

As part of the workshop on district-level reporting, the committee asked representatives from NAGB, NCES, ETS, and Westat to discuss the technical issues related to sampling and scoring methodologies and the policy issues related to participation and reporting decisions. The text below summarizes the information provided by NAEP's sponsors and contractors.

Proposed Sampling Design for Districts

In preparation for the workshop, NCES and Westat provided two documents that outlined the proposed sampling plans for district-level reporting (Rust, 1999; National Center for Education Statistics, 1995). For state NAEP, the sample design involves two-stage stratified samples. Schools are selected at the first stage, and students are selected at the second stage. The typical state sample size is 3,000 students per grade and subject, with 30 students per school. The sample sizes desired for district results would be roughly one-quarter that required for states (750 sampled students at 25 schools, to yield 500 participants at 25 schools). This sample size would be expected to produce standard errors for districts that are about twice the size of standard errors for the state.

Districts that desired to report mean proficiencies by background characteristics—such as race, ethnicity, type of courses taken, home-related variables, instructional variables, and teacher variables—would need sample sizes approximately one-half of their corresponding state sample sizes, or approximately 1,500 students from a minimum of 50 schools. For reporting, the "rule of 62" would apply, meaning that disaggregated results would be provided only for groups with at least 62 students (National Assessment Governing Board, 1995b: Guideline 3).

At the workshop, Richard Valliant, associate director of Westat's Statistical Group, further outlined the sampling requirements for districts. Valliant described the "sparse state" option, that would require fewer schools but would sample more students at the selected schools, and the "small state" option, that would reduce the number of students tested per school. Both options would still require 500 participating students. These sample sizes would allow for the reporting of scaled scores, achievement levels, and percentages of students at or above a given level for the entire district, but would probably not allow for stable estimates of performance for subgroups of the sample.

Peggy Carr, associate commissioner in the Assessment Division at NCES, described two additional alternatives under consideration, the "enhanced district sampling plan" and the "analytic approach." The enhanced district sampling plan would reconfigure the state sampling design so that sufficient numbers of schools were sampled for interested districts. This plan might require oversampling at the district level and applying appropriate weights to schools, and perhaps districts, during analysis. The analytic approach, according to Carr, would allow districts to access existing data in order to identify districts like themselves and compare analytic results. Carr noted that development of details about this option were still under way.

Scoring Methodolgy

During the workshop, Nancy Allen, director of NAEP analysis and research at ETS, described the scoring methodology currently used for NAEP and explained how procedures would be adapted to generate district-level results. Allen reminded participants that ability estimates are not computed for individuals because the number of items to which any given student responds is insufficient to produce a reliable performance estimate. She described procedures used to generate the likely ability distributions for individuals, based on their background characteristics and responses to NAEP items (the conditioning procedures), and to randomly draw five ability estimates (plausible values) from these distributions. She noted that for state NAEP, the conditioning procedures utilize information on the characteristics of all test takers in the state.

Participants and committee members raised questions about the information that would be included in the conditioning models for districts. For example, would the models be based on the characteristics of the state or the characteristics of the district? If models were based on the characteristics of the state, and the characteristics of the state differed from those of the district, would that affect the estimates of performance? Allen responded that the conditioning models rely on information about the relationships (covariation) between performance on test items and background characteristics. According to Allen, sometimes the compositional characteristics of the state and a district will differ with respect to background variables, but the relationships between cognitive performance and background characteristics may not differ. Nevertheless, Allen stressed that they were still exploring various models for calculating estimates at the district level, including some that condition on district characteristics.

Given the potential bias in proficiency estimates that could result from a possibly erroneous conditioning model, the committee offers the following recommendation regarding conditioning procedures.

RECOMMENDATION 3-1: If the decision is made to move forward with providing district-level results, NAEP's sponsors should collect empirical evidence on the most appropriate pro-

cedures for improving the accuracy of estimates of achievement using demographic and background variables (conditioning and plausible values technology). Conditioning is
most defensible when based on district-level background variables. Empirical evidence should be gathered before selecting
an alternate procedure, supporting its acceptability.

Participation Decisions

Roy Truby, executive director of NAGB, told participants that when
Congress lifted the ban on below-state reporting, it neglected to include
language in the law that clarified the roles of states and districts in making
participation decisions. In 1998, when NCES offered results to the naturally occurring districts, the agency sent letters to both the districts and
their respective states. Based on legal advice from the Department of
Education's Office of General Counsel, the agency determined that state
officials, not district officials, would make decisions about release of results.
In at least one case, there appeared to be a conflict in which the state wanted
the data released, but the district did not. NAGB members were concerned
that the districts were not told when they agreed to participate in 1998
NAEP that results for their districts might be released. Because of this
ambiguity about decision-making procedures, NAGB passed the following
resolution (National Assessment Governing Board, 1999d):

> Since the policy on release of district-level results did not envision a disagree-
> ment between state and district officials, the Governing Board hereby sus-
> pends implementation of this policy, pending legislation which would pro-
> vide that the release of district-level NAEP results must be approved by both
> the district and state involved.

The committee asked workshop participants to discuss their opinions
about the entity (states or districts) that should have decision-making
authority over participation and release of data. In general, district representatives believed that the participating entity should make participation
decisions, while state representatives believed that the decision should lie
with the state. Others thought that the entity that paid for participation
should have decision-making authority. However, speakers stressed that
the most pertinent issue was not about participation but about public
release of results. Under the Freedom of Information Act, district results
would be subject to public release once they were compiled.

REACTIONS FROM WORKSHOP PARTICIPANTS

Workshop participants discussed technical and policy issues for district-level NAEP and made a number of observations. They are discussed next.

Comparisons Among Similar Districts

Like Selden (1991), some workshop participants found that district-level reporting would enable useful and important comparisons. Several state and district officials liked the idea of being able to make comparisons among similar districts. District officials reported that often others in the state do not understand the challenges they face, and comparisons with similar districts across state boundaries would enable them to evaluate their performance given their particular circumstances. For instance, some districts are confronting significant population growth that affects their available resources. Others, such as large urban districts, have larger populations of groups that tend to perform less well on achievement tests. District officials believed that if performance could be compared among districts with similar characteristics, state officials might be more likely to set more reasonable and achievable expectations. Further, they noted that this practice might allow them to identify districts performing better than expected, given their demographics, and attention could focus on determining instructional practices that work well.

A number of workshop participants were worried about the uses that might be made of district-level results. Some expressed concern that results would be used for accountability purposes and to chastise or reward school districts for their students' performance. Using district-level results as part of accountability programs would be especially problematic if the content and skills covered by NAEP were not aligned with local and state curricula. Officials from some of the larger urban areas also argued that they already know that their children do not perform as well as students in more affluent suburban districts. Having another set of assessment results would provide yet another opportunity for the press and others to criticize them.

Other state and district officials commented that states' varied uses of assessments may confound comparisons. While districts may seem comparable based on their demographics, they may in fact be very different, because of the context associated with state assessment programs. States differ in the emphases they place on test results, the uses of the scores, and the amounts and kinds of attention results receive from the press. These factors play a significant role in setting the stage for the testing and can make comparisons misleading, even when districts appear similar because of their student populations.

External Validation

Some state and district officials were attracted to the prospect of having a means for external validation. They find NAEP to be a stable external measure of achievement against which they could compare their state and local assessment results. However, some also noted that attempts to obtain external validation for state assessments can create a double bind. When the findings from external measures corroborate state assessment results, no questions are asked. However, when state or local assessment results and external measures (such as state NAEP) differ, assessment directors are often asked, "Which set of results is correct?" Explaining and accounting for these differences can be challenging. Having multiple indicators that suggest different findings can lead to public confusion about students' achievement.

These challenges are particularly acute when a state or local assessment is similar, but not identical, to NAEP. For example, some state assessment programs have adopted the NAEP descriptors (advanced, proficient, and basic) for their achievement levels. However, their descriptions of performance differ in important ways from the NAEP descriptions. NAEP's definition of "proficient," for instance, may encompass different skills than the state's definition, creating problems for those who must explain and interpret the two sets of test results.

Some district and state officials expressed concern about the alignment between their curricula and the material tested on NAEP. Their state and local assessments are part of an accountability system that includes instruction, assessment, and evaluation. NAEP results would be less meaningful if they were based on content and skills not covered by their instructional programs. Attempts to use NAEP as a means of external validation for the state assessment is problematic when the state assessment is aligned with instruction and NAEP is not, particularly if results from the different assessments suggest different findings about students' achievement.

In addition, confusion arises when NAEP results are released at the same time as state or local assessment results. State and local results are timely, generally reporting data for a cohort while it is still in the particular grade. For instance, when reports are published on the achievement of a school system's fourth graders, they represent the cohort currently in fourth grade. When NAEP results are published, they are for some previous year's fourth graders. This again can lead to public confusion over students' academic accomplishments.

Supplemental Assessments

An appealing feature to state and district officials participating in the workshop was the possibility of having assessment results in subject areas and grades not tested by their state or local programs. Although state and local programs generally test students in reading and mathematics, not all provide assessments of all of the subject areas NAEP assesses, such as writing, science, civics, and foreign languages. Some participants liked the idea of receiving results for twelfth graders, a grade not usually tested by state assessments. Also, NAEP collects background data that many states do not have the resources to collect. Some workshop participants have found the background data to be exceedingly useful and would look forward to receiving reports that would associate district-level performance with background and environmental data.

Lack of Program Details

Workshop participants were bothered by the lack of specifications about district-level reporting. Even though the committee asked NAEP's sponsors to describe the plans and features of district-level reporting, many of the details have not yet been determined. In responding to questions put to them about district-level reporting, many participating state and district officials formulated their own assumptions and reacted to the program they thought might be enacted. For instance, as mentioned above, they assumed that assessments would be offered in the subject areas and grades available for national NAEP; however, district NAEP has currently only been associated with state NAEP. Hence, only reading, mathematics, writing, and science would be available and only in grades 4 and 8 (not 12). Those that looked forward to receiving data summarized by background characteristics would likely be disappointed given the sample sizes required to obtain such information.

Other state and district officials commented that their reactions to the propositions set forth by NAEP's sponsors would depend upon the details.

Some of their questions included: How much would it cost to participate in district-level NAEP? Who would pay for the costs? How would it be administered—centrally, as with national NAEP, or locally, as with state NAEP? What type of information would be included in the reports? How long would it take to receive results? Would district-level results require the same time lag for reporting as national and state NAEP? The answers to these questions would determine whether or not they would be interested in participating.

Of concern to a number of participants, particularly to representatives from the Council of Chief State School Officers, was the issue of small districts. The sampling specifications described at the workshop indicated that districts would need at least 25 schools in a given grade level to receive reports. Technical experts present at the workshop wondered if sufficient thought had been given to the sample size specifications. If the district met the sample size requirements for students (i.e., at least 750 students), the number of schools should not matter. In state and national NAEP, there is considerable variation in average achievement levels across schools, and only a small percentage of schools are sampled and tested. A target of 100 schools was set to be sure that the between-school variation was adequately captured. In district NAEP, there would be fewer schools and less variability between schools. In smaller districts, all schools might be included in the sample, thereby eliminating completely the portion of sampling error associated with between-school differences. Technical experts and others at the workshop encouraged NCES and Westat to pursue sampling specifications and focus on the estimated overall accuracy of results rather than on specifying an arbitrary minimum number of schools based on current procedures for State or National NAEP.

Others questioned how "district" might be defined and if district consortia would be allowed. Some participants were familiar with the First in the World consortium, formed by a group of districts in Illinois to participate and receive results from the Third International Mathematics and Science Study. They wondered if such district consortia would be permitted for NAEP.

SUGGESTIONS FOR NAEP'S SPONSORS

The reporting system that is the subject of this chapter would create a new program with new NAEP products. One of the objectives for convening the committee's workshop on district-level reporting was to learn about the factors that would affect states' and districts' interest in this new product. After listening to workshop participants' comments and reviewing the available materials, the committee finds that many of the details regarding district-level reporting have not been thoroughly considered or laid out. District officials, state officials, and other NAEP users—the potential users of the new product—had a difficult time responding to questions about the product's desirability because a clear conception of its characteristics was not available. The most important issues requiring resolution are described below.

Clarify the Goals and Objectives

The goals and objectives of district-level reporting were not apparent from written materials or from information provided during the workshop. Some workshop participants spoke of using tests for accountability purposes, questioning whether NAEP could be used in this way or not. They discussed the amount of testing in their schools and stressed that new testing would need to be accompanied by new (and better) information. However, some had difficulty identifying what new and better information might result from district-level NAEP data. Their comments might have been different, and perhaps more informative, if they had a clear idea of the purposes and objectives for district-level reporting. An explicit statement is needed that specifies the goals and objectives for district-level reporting and presents a logical argument for how the program is expected to achieve the desired outcomes.

Evaluate Costs and Benefits

What would districts and states receive? When would they receive the information? How much would it cost? What benefits would be realized from the information? Workshop participants responded to questions about their interests in the program without having answers to these questions, though many said that their interest would depend on the answers. They need information on the types of reports to be prepared along with the associated costs. They need to know about the time lag for reporting. Would reports be received in time to use in their decision and policy making or would the time delays be such as to render the information useless?

Costs and benefits must be considered in terms of teachers' and students' time and effort. State systems already extensively test fourth and eighth graders. If time is to be taken away from instruction for the purpose of additional testing, the benefits of the testing need to be laid out. Will additional testing amplify the information already provided? Or will the information be redundant to that provided from current tests? Will the redundancy make it useful for external validation? Such information needs to be provided in order for NAEP's sponsors to assess actual levels of interest in the program.

Evaluate Participation Levels

During the workshop, many spoke of the value of being able to make inter-district comparisons based on districts with like characteristics. However, this use of the results assumes that sufficient numbers of districts will participate. Previous experiences with district-level reporting resulted in a relatively low level of interest: between 10 and 12 interested districts in 1996 and virtually none in 1998.

Meaningful comparisons, as defined by demographic, political, and other contextual variables of importance to districts require a variety of other districts with district-level reports. Having only a handful of districts that meet the sampling criteria may limit one of the most fundamental appeals of district-level reporting—that is, carefully selecting others with which to compare results. Thus, if making comparisons is the primary objective for receiving district-level reports, the targeted districts must feel secure in knowing that there are sister districts also completing the necessary procedures for receiving district-level results. The extent of participation will limit the ability to make the desired comparisons.

Consider the Impact of Raising the Stakes

A concern expressed when state NAEP was first implemented related to the potential for higher stakes to be associated with reporting data for smaller units. The message from several workshop speakers (particularly district representatives) was that district-level reports would raise the stakes associated with NAEP and change the way NAEP results are used. An evaluation should be conducted on the effects of higher stakes, particularly as they relate to the types of inferences that may be made.

CONCLUSIONS AND RECOMMENDATIONS

It was impossible for the committee to gauge actual interest in district-level reporting because too little information—such as program objectives, specifications, and costs—was available to potential users. When developing a new product, it is common to seek reactions from potential users to identify design features that will make it more attractive. The reactions of potential users and the responses from product designers tend to produce a series of interactions like "Tell me what the new product is and I will tell you if I like it," versus "Tell me what you would like the product to be and I will make sure it will have those characteristics." During the committee's workshop, state and district representatives were put in the position of responding to the latter question. Here, the developer is asking the user to do some of the design work. Often times the user is not knowledgeable enough to give sound design recommendations. Instead, the product designer needs to present concrete prototypes to get credible evaluative reaction. And, the developer should expect several iterations of prototype design and evaluation before the design stabilizes at a compromise between users' needs and what is practically possible. This is the type of process required before ideas and products associated with district-level reporting can progress.

RECOMMENDATION 3-2: Market research emphasizing both needs analysis and product analysis is necessary to evaluate the level of interest in district-level reporting. The decision to move ahead with district-level reporting should be based on the results of market research conducted by an independent market-research organization. If market research suggests that there is little or no interest in district-level reporting, NAEP's sponsors should not continue to invest NAEP's limited resources pursuing district-level reporting.

4

Market-Basket Reporting

Market-basket reporting for NAEP has been proposed as a way to summarize academic achievement on a representative collection of NAEP test items. The objectives for market-basket reporting are twofold: to summarize performance in a way that is more comfortable to users; and to release the collection of items so that users would have a concrete reference for the meaning of the scores (National Assessment Governing Board, 1997). In addition, the market-basket approach would make it possible to track performance over time to document changes in students' academic accomplishments. The ultimate goal is to better communicate what students in the United States are expected to know and be able to do, according to the subject areas, content and skills, and grade levels assessed on NAEP.

The earliest references to market-basket reporting of NAEP assessments appeared in the "Policy Statement on Redesigning the National Assessment of Educational Progress" (National Assessment Governing Board, 1996) and in the Design and Feasibility Team's Report to NAGB (Forsyth et al., 1996). These documents referred to market-basket reporting as "domain-score reporting" where a "goodly number of test questions are developed that encompass the subject, and student results are reported as a percentage of the 'domain' that students 'know and can do'" (National Assessment Governing Board, 1996:13). According to these documents, the general idea of a NAEP market basket draws on an image similar to the Consumer Price Index (CPI): a collection of test questions representative of some larger content domain; and an easily-understood index to summarize performance on the items. These writings generally refer to two components of the NAEP market basket, the collection of items and the summary index. The documents consider collections of items that are large (e.g., too many items to be administered to a single student in its entirety) or small (e.g., small enough to be considered an administrable test form). They consider percent correct scores as the metric for summarizing performance on the collection of items, a metric NAEP's sponsors believe is widely understood (National Assessment Governing Board, 1997). Figure 1-1 (see Chapter 1) provides a pictorial description for the NAEP market basket and its various components.

Perceptions about the configuration and uses for the NAEP market basket are not uniform. NAGB's current policies address the short form version of a market basket, stating that its goal is to "enable faster, more understandable initial reporting of results" and to allow states access to test instruments to obtain NAEP results in years when particular subjects are not scheduled (National Assessment Governing Board, 1999a). Educators from both the state and local level who participated in the committee's workshops envisioned NAEP market-basket forms as short forms that could be used as an alternative to or in connection with their local assessments possibly for the purpose of comparing local assessment results with NAEP results (National Research Council, 2000). At the committee's workshop and in his writings on domain score reporting, Bock (1997) described the market basket as a tool for sampling student knowledge over the entire domain of any given content area. Under Bock's conception, the focus would extend beyond what is measured by NAEP and would support score inferences that provide information about how a student would perform on the larger domain. If one were to draw a direct parallel between the CPI, an economic index that summarizes actual consumer purchases, one could reasonably expect a market basket positioned as an educational index to measure and report exactly what it is that students are learning.

The intent of this chapter is to explore various conceptions of market-basket reporting and discuss issues associated with NAEP's implementation of such a reporting mechanism. We address the following study questions: (1) What is market-basket reporting? (2) What information needs might be served by market-basket reporting for NAEP? (3) Are market-basket reports likely to be relevant and accurate enough to meet these needs? This chapter deals more broadly with market-basket reporting, while the next chapter focuses specifically on the short form.

The first section of this chapter lays out the psychometric issues that should be considered in connection with market-basket reporting. This is followed by a description of the pilot study currently under way at ETS and comments made by participants in the committee's workshop. The final section of the chapter presents details on the methodology for constructing and reporting results for the CPI market basket.

STUDY APPROACH

During the course of the study, the committee reviewed the literature and the policy guidelines pertaining to market-basket reporting, including the following documents: Design and Feasibility Team's report to NAGB (Forsyth et al., 1996); ETS's proposal (Educational Testing Service, 1998); various studies on domain score reporting (Bock, 1997; Bock, Thissen, & Zimowski, 1997; Pommerich & Nicewander, 1998); and policy guidelines included in the 1996 NAEP Redesign (National Assessment Governing Board, 1996) and in NAEP Design 2000-2010 policy (National Assessment Governing Board, 1999a). In addition, the committee listened to presentations by NAGB and NCES staff about market-basket reporting.

As mentioned in Chapter 1, the committee held a workshop on market-basket reporting which provided a forum for discussions with representatives of the organizations involved in setting policy for and operating NAEP (NAGB and NCES) along with individuals from ETS, the contractual agency that works on NAEP. In preparation for the workshop, NCES, NAGB, and ETS staff prepared the following papers:

1. *A Market Basket for NAEP: Policies and Objectives of the National Assessment Governing Board* by Roy Truby, executive director of NAGB
2. *Simplifying the Interpretation of NAEP Results With Market Baskets and Shortened Forms of NAEP* by Andrew Kolstad, senior technical advisor for the Assessment Division at NCES
3. *Evidentiary Relationships among Data-Gathering Methods and Reporting Scales In Surveys of Educational Achievement* by Robert Mislevy, distinguished research scholar with ETS
4. *NAEP's Year 2000 Market Basket Study: What Do We Expect to Learn?* by John Mazzeo, executive director of ETS's School and College Services

Individuals representing a variety of perspectives—education policy, assessment, curriculum and instruction, measurement, and the press—reacted to the ideas presented by NAEP's sponsors and contractors. Because the conception of the market basket has often been illustrated through analogies to the CPI market basket, we also arranged for a briefing on the CPI from a representative of the Bureau of Labor Statistics. Approximately 40 individuals participated in the workshop, and the results were summarized and published (National Research Council, 2000).

PSYCHOMETRIC CONSIDERATIONS FOR THE NAEP MARKET BASKET

While the idea behind market-basket reporting is to produce more easily understood test results, the "behind-the-scenes" technology required to enable such reporting methodology is quite complex. During the workshop, Robert Mislevy laid the conceptual groundwork for the technical and measurement issues involved in market-basket reporting (Mislevy, 2000); Andrew Kolstad traced the history of NAEP reporting practices (Kolstad, 2000); and John Mazzeo described features of the pilot study currently under way on the market basket. In the section that follows, we draw from the ideas presented by Mislevy, Kolstad, and Mazzeo and from other sources to delineate the psychometric issues that must be addressed in designing a NAEP market basket.

The Market Basket Domain

Perhaps the most critical issue for a market basket is determining the domain to be measured. For the current pilot study, the market basket domain is limited to the pool of existing or newly constructed NAEP items (Mazzeo, 2000). Such a domain might be selected as most desirable, but it is not the only way to define the market basket. Figure 4-1 depicts several key factors that must be considered.

For any given content area, the first stage in developing instruction and assessment programs is delimitation of the targeted range of knowledge, skills, and objectives. In most cases, the range of material is too broad to be covered by a given instructional and assessment plan, forcing educators to choose what they consider most important for students to know and learn. Under its broadest definition, the domain would include knowledge and skills: (1) deemed important by content experts; (2) covered by text-

FIGURE 4-1 Critical Factors for Market Basket Development

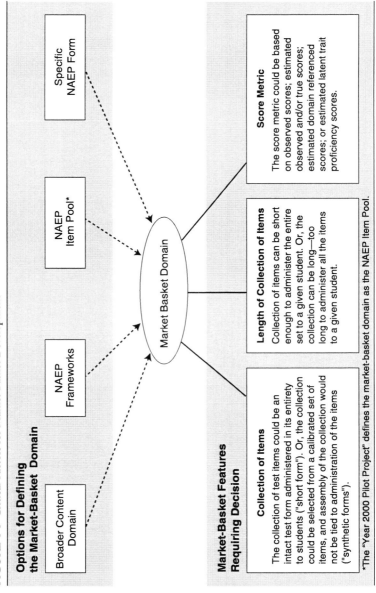

Options for Defining the Market-Basket Domain

Broader Content Domain

NAEP Frameworks

NAEP Item Pool*

Specific NAEP Form

Market Basket Domain

Market-Basket Features Requiring Decision

Collection of Items

The collection of test items could be an intact test form administered in its entirety to students ("short form"). Or, the collection could be selected from a calibrated set of items, and assembly of the collection would not be tied to administration of the items ("synthetic forms").

Length of Collection of Items

Collection of items can be short enough to administer the entire set to a given student. Or, the collection can be long—too long to administer all the items to a given student.

Score Metric

The score metric could be based on observed scores; estimated observed and/or true scores; estimated domain referenced scores; or estimated latent trait proficiency scores.

*The "Year 2000 Pilot Project" defines the market-basket domain as the NAEP Item Pool.

books and other instructional material; (3) specified by state and local curriculum guides; (4) actually taught in the classroom; and (5) believed to be critical by the larger public. NAEP's use of matrix sampling allows it to define the domain broadly, as is evident in the NAEP frameworks. The frameworks were selected through a broad-based consensus process to balance current educational practice and reform recommendations (National Research Council, 1999b).

Because the length of any assessment is constrained by time, the collection of items a student takes can only be expected to be a sample from the domain. As with other tests, frameworks guide item and task development for NAEP so that performance on the test items can support inferences about the domain. The intent is to provide a reference for test construction that assures the final assessment will be representative of the defined domain.

In constructing the market basket, the alignment of the item pool to the framework, as well as the framework's representation of the broad domain, have a substantial impact on the potential validity of inferences based on market-basket scores. Given that the pilot study defines the domain as the pool of existing and newly constructed NAEP items (Mazzeo, 2000), inferences from market-basket scores to the NAEP frameworks will rely on how well the item pool represents the frameworks. The Committee on the Evaluation of National and State Assessments of Educational Progress (National Research Council, 1999b:132), evaluated the fit of NAEP items to the frameworks. They concluded:

> In general, the assessment item pools are reasonably reflective of the goals for distributions of items set forth, in the framework matrices, particularly in the content-area dimensions in mathematics and science.

> However, the presence of standards-based goals in the frameworks and the general fit of the assessment item pools to categories in the major framework dimensions do not ensure that the goals of the framework have been successfully translated into assessment materials. Several lines of evidence indicate that NAEP's assessments, as currently constructed and scored, do not adequately assess some of the most valued aspects of the frameworks, particularly with respect to assessing the more complex cognitive skills and levels and types of students' understanding.

Thus, it is not clear that defining the domain as the pool of existing or newly developed NAEP items will result in a set of items for the market basket that adequately represent the frameworks.

The Basis for Market-Basket Reporting

To define the basis for market-basket reporting, two decisions must be made. The first relates to the set of items that set the scale for the percent correct or percent of maximum score; the second pertains to the method used to collect the data that are summarized using the market-basket approach. The set of test items used to define the market basket could either be administered to students as part of data collection, or they could be selected from a calibrated set of items solely for the purpose of defining the score scale for reporting performance on the market basket. In the former case, the set of items could take the shape of an intact test form administered in its entirety to students. Given time constraints for test administration, an administrable form would need to be relatively short, short enough to administer during a 40- or 50-minute testing session. We refer to this sort of a collection of items as a "short form." In the latter case, the set of items could be assembled to represent the content and skill domain, but assembly of the collection would not be tied to administration of the items. That is, the items would be administered as part of NAEP but not necessarily in a form that would be used for reporting. This conception of the market basket—a collection of items that is never administered in its entirety as an intact test form—is called a "synthetic" form. Synthetic forms can be long or short.

Synthetic forms can be developed to meet a variety of reporting goals. One alternative would be to use a very large pool of items that is too large to administer to any individual. This pool would yield better representation of the NAEP framework, but it could provide more information than can easily be assimilated by the audiences for NAEP results. Alternatively, a synthetic form could be a smaller set of items that represents the NAEP framework in a more limited way and that could be used as a constant reference over time for tracking performance. Since the form would be short, it would not provide information about the nuances of the NAEP framework, only the major points.

A third alternative could be a collection of synthetic short forms, which together would provide a more detailed representation of the NAEP framework than would a single short form. This would overcome the limitations in coverage of a single short form. Using multiple forms, however, introduces the complication of comparing results across test forms that are not identical.

Thus, the data that form the basis for market-basket reporting can be collected using the large pool of items as is currently done with NAEP, or via a short form or multiple short forms. The means for transforming the scores to the reporting metric will vary depending on the data collection method.

Constructing Multiple Market-Basket Forms

As stated above, market-basket reporting could be based on a single short form. Given the breadth of the NAEP frameworks, however, short forms necessarily will be limited in the way that they represent the NAEP frameworks. To overcome the limitations in coverage of a single short form, multiple market-basket forms can be constructed to be either technically parallel (each measures similar content and skills) or arbitrary (each measures different sets of content and skills). Parallel test forms are commonly used in large-scale achievement testing, while arbitrary forms are typical of NAEP.

Arbitrary test forms measure the same general domain of content and skills, but they are not necessarily constructed to be comparable. They can be expected to have varying test length, use different item formats, and differentially sample the content domain. The test parameters from each form will also differ.

Parallel forms, on the other hand, more consistently sample the domain for a given group of examinees. However, the construction of parallel test forms presents a developmental challenge. According to Stanley (1971: 405):

> The best guarantee of parallelism for two test forms would seem to be that a complete and detailed set of specifications for the test be prepared in advance of any final test construction. The set of specification should indicate item types, difficulty level of items, procedures and standards for item selection and refinement, and distribution of items with regard to the content to be covered, specified in as much detail as seems feasible. If each test form is then built to conform to the outline, while at the same time care is taken to avoid identity or detailed overlapping of content, the two resulting test forms should be truly comparable.

Depending on the degree to which parallelism is actually obtained, forms can be classified as classically parallel, tau-equivalent, or congeneric (Feldt & Brennan, 1989). The differences among these classifications pertain to the distributions of true scores, error scores, and observed scores on the forms. [1]

To some extent, the type of forms used in data collection will directly affect the score distributions for the test. Knowing how scores are expected to be distributed serves as an indicator for selection of appropriate statistical tools for estimating and reporting student performance. With rare exception, the type of test forms used for NAEP have been arbitrary forms; coupled with matrix sampling, their use has necessitated complex statistical techniques for estimating examinee performance (i.e., imputation and conditioning). If the desire is to make comparisons between market-basket results and main NAEP or to make predictions from one to the other, procedures for deriving scores for NAEP market baskets will be similarly complex. If there is no intention to compare results with main NAEP or to predict performance on one from the other, forms used to facilitate market-basket reporting need not follow the path of NAEP and can be constructed to yield more easily derivable and interpretable information.

Statistical Methods for Linking Scores from Multiple Test Forms

If multiple test forms are used, student performance across the forms will likely differ. Even if the forms were constructed in a manner intended to yield parallel forms (i.e., similar in content, format, difficulty, and length), differences in difficulties will be expected. Equating procedures can be used to adjust for differences in difficulty levels (though not to align content or make up for test length differences) and will yield scores that can be used interchangeably across forms (Kolen & Brennan, 1995). Percent correct scores based on different forms can, thus, be equated, and adjusted percent correct scores reported.

---

[1]Classically parallel forms must, theoretically, yield score distributions with identical means and variances for both observed scores and true scores. Classically parallel forms share a common metric. Tau-equivalent forms have the same mix of items but may differ slightly with regard to the numbers of items. Tau-equivalent measures can yield different error variances and observed score variances. True scores as well as their variances are constant across tau-equivalent forms as long as forms do not vary in length in any meaningful way. Congeneric forms include the same essential mix of knowledge and skills but may differ in terms of the number and difficulty of the items. The observed score distributions from congeneric forms may have different characteristics that may in part result from variations in test length.

Since arbitrary forms can consist of a different mix of item types and can vary in test length and difficulty levels, scores based on arbitrary forms must be linked using calibration techniques, rather than equating procedures. Further, the precision with which scores on arbitrary forms are estimated can vary both across forms and across student proficiency levels within a form. Given these differences among forms, Item Response Theory (IRT) models are most often used for linking scores from different forms.

Comparisons between Market-Basket Scores and NAEP Performance

Market-basket reporting requires some method for placing NAEP results on the market-basket score scale. This can be accomplished directly by administering one or more market-basket short forms to a statistically representative sample of the NAEP examinee population. This approach will not work for the long-form market basket, however, because the number of items is too great to administer to an individual student.

An alternative approach is to project NAEP results from a separate data collection onto the score scale defined by a market-basket form. The form can be either an administrable short form or one of a variety of synthetic forms. The methodology used for projection is statistically intensive because of complexities in the dimensional structure of some NAEP frameworks (e.g., the multiple scales) as well as the IRT and plausible values methodologies used for the analysis.

Score Metrics

There are several score metrics that can be considered for market-basket reporting, each of which poses challenges in terms of providing NAEP's audiences with a more easily understood summary of performance. The proposed score metrics are: (1) observed scores, (2) estimated observed and/or true scores, (3) estimated domain referenced scores, and (4) estimated latent trait proficiency scores.

Observed Scores

The observed score metric is based on a tally of the number of right answers or the number of points received. The most direct method for obtaining observed scores is to administer one or more short forms to an appropriate sample of students. The observed score that has most frequently been suggested for market-basket reporting is the percent correct score. Observed scores can be quickly converted to a percent correct or percent of maximum score by adding the number correct on the multiple-choice items and the points received on the constructed response items and then dividing the sum by the total number of possible points. Observed scores have the problem of being tied to the composition and difficulty of the collection of items on the test form. Under a configuration in which multiple forms were used, a method (equating or calibration) would be needed to adjust scores for these form differences so that the scores would have the same interpretation.

At first blush, percent correct scores seem to be a simple, straightforward, and intuitively appealing way to increase public understanding of NAEP results. However, they present complexities of their own. First, NAEP contains a mix of multiple-choice and constructed response items. Multiple-choice items are awarded one point if answered correctly and zero points if answered incorrectly. Answers to constructed response items are awarded a varying number of points. For some constructed response questions, 6 is the top score; for others, 3 is the top score. For a given task, more points are awarded to answers that demonstrate greater proficiency. Therefore, in order to come up with a simple sum of the number of correct responses to test items that include constructed response items, one would need to understand the judgment behind "correct answers." What would it mean to get a "correct answer" on a constructed response item? Receiving all points? Half of the points? Any score above zero?

As an alternative, the percent correct score might be based not on the number of questions but on the total number of points. This presents another complexity, however. Adding the number of points would result in awarding more weight to the constructed response questions than the multiple-choice questions. For example, suppose a constructed response question could receive between 1 and 6 points, with a 2 representing slightly more competence in the area than a 1 but clearly not enough competence to get a 6. Compare a score of 2 out of 6 possible points on this item versus a multiple-choice item where the top score for a correct answer is 1. A simple sum would give twice as much weight to the barely correct constructed response item than to a correct multiple-choice item. This might be reasonable if the constructed response questions required a level of skill higher than the multiple-choice questions, such that a score of 2 on the former actually represented twice as much skill as a score of 1 on the latter, but this is not the case for NAEP questions. Hence, some type of weighting scheme is needed. Yet, that weighting also would introduce complexity to the percent correct metric.

Estimated True Score

Reporting on a true score metric involves making a prediction from the observed score to the *expected* true score (it is a *predicted* score, since an individual's true score is never known). For a NAEP short form, the prediction would be based on the sample of administered items. A similar prediction would be made for the estimated observed score based on a longer form of which a given student takes only a portion of items. Estimated true scores could be derived from techniques aligned with either classical test theory or IRT. Reporting on an estimated true score or estimated observed score metric means working with predictive distributions of these scores which requires statistical procedures that are more complex than those for reporting observed number correct or percent correct scores.

Estimated Domain Score

As defined by Bock (1997), the estimated domain referenced score involves expressing scale scores in terms of the expected percent correct on a larger collection of items that are representative of the specified domain. The expected percent correct can be calculated for any given scale score using IRT methods (see Bock et al., 1997). This calculation would involve transforming observed scores, based on an assessment of part of the domain, to an expected percent correct score. While derivation of this score would require complex procedures, it would result in scores on the metric (e.g., percent correct) that NAEP's sponsors consider more intuitively appealing than an IRT proficiency score (Kolstad, 2000).

Estimated Proficiency Score

IRT-based procedures for estimating proficiency yield estimates referred to as "latent trait estimates." Use of the latent trait metric requires estimation of the latent trait distribution. NAEP currently estimates latent trait distributions that are converted to scaled score distributions for reporting. Estimating the latent trait distribution also involves complicated transformations from observed scores but has the advantage that, when

IRT assumptions are met, the distributions generalize beyond the specific set of administered items. Market-basket reports could use the latent trait (theta) metric, or latent trait scores could be converted to scaled scores, but reporting on this metric would not ameliorate the interpretation problems associated with the current NAEP reporting scale.

THE YEAR 2000 PILOT STUDY ON
MARKET BASKET REPORTING

The market-basket pilot study, currently under way at ETS, was designed with three goals in mind: (1) to produce and evaluate a market-basket report of NAEP results; (2) to gain experience with constructing short forms; and (3) to conduct research on the methodological and technical issues associated with implementing a market-basket reporting system (Mazzeo, 2000). The study involves the construction of two fourth-grade mathematics test forms, also referred to as *administrable* or *short* forms. Under one configuration for market-basket reporting, one of these forms would be released as the market basket set of exemplar items, and the other would be treated as a secure form for states and districts to administer as they see fit. The pilot study also investigates preparation and release of the longer version of the market basket. ETS researchers plan to simulate a longer synthetic form of the market basket by combining the two short forms. Because no student will have taken both short forms, scores for the long form will be derived from performance on the items and the relationships across the forms.

The test developers hope that the study will serve as a learning experience regarding the construction of alternate NAEP short forms, since short forms might be used by NAEP even without the move to market-basket reporting. Whereas creating intact test forms is a standard part of most testing programs, this is not the case with NAEP. NAEP's current system for developing and field testing items was set up to support the construction of a system of arbitrary test forms in an efficient manner and does not yet have guidelines for constructing market baskets or intact tests.

A NAEP test development committee handled construction of the short forms. They were instructed to identify a set of secure NAEP items that were high quality exemplars of the pool and to select items that matched the pool with respect to content, process, format, and statistical specifications. The committee constructed two forms that could be administered within a 45-minute time period, one consisting of 31 items, the other containing 33 items. The items were organized into three distinct blocks, each given during separately timed 15-minute test sessions. One of the short forms consisted of previously administered secure items; the other consisted of new items. Both forms were given to a random sample of 8,000 students during the NAEP 2000 administration. The forms were spiraled[2] with previously administered NAEP materials to enable linking to NAEP.

The study's sponsors expect the research to yield three products: (1) one or more secure short forms; (2) a research report intended for technical audiences that examines test development and data analytic issues associated with the implementation of market-basket reporting; and (3) a report intended for general audiences.

ETS researchers will continue to study alternative analysis and data collection methods. One of their planned studies involves conducting separate analyses of the year-2000 data using methods appropriate for arbitrary forms, methods appropriate for congeneric forms, and methods appropriate for parallel forms. Each of these sets of analyses will produce results in an observed score metric as well as a true score metric. Comparisons of results from the other approaches to the results from the arbitrary forms will provide concrete information about which data gathering options are most viable for the market-basket concept. These comparisons will evaluate the degree of similarity among the sets of results based on the stronger models, which use congeneric or parallel forms and involve less complex analytic procedures, and results from the arbitrary forms, which make the weakest assumptions but involve the most complicated analyses. If the results are similar, the simpler data collection and analytic procedures may be acceptable. In addition, comparing observed score and true score results for each of the approaches will inform decisions about which type of reporting scale should be used.

The year-2000 study will also evaluate the potential benefit of using longer market baskets. The 31-item short forms were chosen to minimize school and student burden and to increase the chances of obtaining school participation in NAEP. Other decisions regarding test length could also be

---

[2]Spiraling is an approach to form distribution in which one copy of each different form is handed out before spiraling down to a second copy of each form and then a third and so forth. The goals of this approach are to achieve essentially random assignment of students to forms while ensuring that approximately equal numbers of students complete each form.

made, such as the domain score reporting approach (Bock, 1997). (See Chapter 5 for a description of this approach.) Clearly, a longer collection of items would permit more adequate domain coverage and produce more reliable results.

WORKSHOP PARTICIPANTS' REACTIONS TO PLANS FOR MARKET-BASKET REPORTING

Large-Scale Release of NAEP Items

Participants in the committee's workshop on market-basket reporting suggested several ways for the market-basket set of items to be used. Test directors and school system administrators found the idea of releasing a representative set of items to be very appealing and maintained this would help to "demystify" NAEP. In their interactions with the public, school officials have found that many of their constituents often question the amount of time devoted to testing and are unsure of how to interpret the results. They believe that the public is not fully aware of the range of material on achievement tests, the skills that students are expected to demonstrate, and the inferences that test results can support. Furthermore, the public does not always see the link between assessment programs and school reform efforts. Helping the public better understand what is being tested and the rationale for testing could do much to garner public support for continuing to gather this information.

The release of NAEP items could also fulfill a second purpose. Even though the market basket set of items would be representative of NAEP, some state testing programs cover content similar to that assessed by NAEP. Therefore, NAEP's release of items could increase understanding of state and local assessments.

Curriculum specialists and school administrators observed that the release of a large number of items could stimulate discussion among teachers regarding the format and content of questions. Review of the items could facilitate discussions about how local curricula (particularly content coverage and the sequencing of course material) compare with the material covered on NAEP. Workshop speakers explained that it is often difficult to draw conclusions about their states' NAEP performance because it is not clear whether the material tested on NAEP is covered by their curricula or at which grade level it is covered.

State and local assessment directors suggested that a large-scale release of NAEP items and related test materials could improve state and local assessment programs. Many judge NAEP items to be of high quality. Allowing test developers to view large amounts of NAEP test materials could have a positive effect on the quality of item design for state and local assessments. Similarly, review of items by teachers could serve to improve classroom-based assessments.

While participants generally saw value in a large-scale release of items, some were concerned about the uses made of the items. Assessment directors and curriculum specialists worried that a large release might unduly influence local and state curricula or assessments. For instance, policy makers and educators concerned about their NAEP performance could attempt to align their curricula more closely with what is tested on NAEP. Because assessment, curricula, and instructional practices form a tightly woven system, making changes to one aspect of the system can have an impact on other aspects. Attempts to align curricula more closely to NAEP could upset the entire instructional program.

Percent Correct Scores

Nearly all speakers were skeptical about using percent correct scores to report performance and were doubtful that it would accomplish its intended purpose. Assessment directors and measurement experts commented that percent correct scores were not as simple as they might seem. For instance, would percent correct be based on the number of correct answers or the number of possible points? Furthermore, how could a percent correct score be compared to the main NAEP scale, given that main NAEP results are not reported on this metric? Several assessment directors commented that they had devoted considerable time to helping users understand achievement-level reporting and felt that their constituencies had become familiar with this reporting mechanism. Percent correct scores would require new interpretative assistance. In addition, while percent correct scores would be associated with the achievement levels (i.e., the percent correct at basic, proficient, and advanced), these percentages may not conform to public beliefs about performance at a given level. The percent correct required to be considered proficient, for instance, could turn out to be lower than the public would expect. Such a discrepancy could damage the public's opinion of NAEP.

CONSTRUCTION OF THE CONSUMER PRICE INDEX MARKET BASKET

During the course of this study, the materials NAEP's sponsors provided to the committee described general ideas for the NAEP market basket but did not present firm proposals for its design. The committee believed it would be instructive to learn about summary indicators used in other fields. Because the NAEP market basket has been linked with the CPI from its inception, the committee thought it would be useful to learn more about how the CPI was constructed and how it might be applied in an educational setting. During the committee's workshop on market-basket reporting, Kenneth Stewart from the Bureau of Labor Statistics (BLS) described the processes and methods used for deriving and utilizing the CPI. Stewart's remarks are summarized below; additional details about the CPI appear in Appendix B.

Background and Current Uses of the CPI

The CPI is a measure of the average change over time in the prices paid by urban consumers in the United States for a fixed basket of goods in a fixed geographic area. The CPI was developed during World War I so that the federal government could establish cost-of-living adjustments for workers in shipbuilding centers. Today, the CPI is the principal source of information concerning trends in consumer prices and inflation in the United States. It is widely used as an economic indicator and a means of adjusting other economic series (e.g., retail sales, hourly earnings) and dollar values used in government programs, such as payments to Social Security recipients and to Federal and military retirees. The BLS currently produces two national indices every month: the CPI for All Urban Consumers and the more narrowly based CPI for Urban Wage Earners and Clerical Workers, which is developed using data from households represented in only certain occupations. In addition to the national indexes, the BLS produces indexes for geographic regions and collective urban areas. Compositions of the regional market baskets generally vary substantially across areas because of differences in purchasing patterns. Thus, these indexes cannot be used for relative comparisons of the level of prices or the cost of living in different geographic areas.

Collection of Data on Consumer Expenditures

The BLS develops the CPI market basket on the basis of detailed information provided by families and individuals about their actual purchases. Information on purchases is gathered from households in the Consumer Expenditure Survey, which consists of two components: an interview survey and a diary survey.[3]   Each component has its own questionnaire and sample.

In the quarterly interview portion of the Consumer Expenditure survey, an interviewer visits every consumer in the sample every 3 months over a 12-month period. The Consumer Expenditure interview survey is designed to collect data on the types of expenditures that respondents can be expected to recall for a period of 3 months or longer. These expenditures include major purchases, such as property, automobiles, and major appliances, and expenses that occur on a regular basis, such as rent, insurance premiums, and utilities. Expenditures incurred on trips are also reported in this survey. The Consumer Expenditure interview survey thus collects detailed data on 60 to 70 percent of total household expenditures. Global estimates—i.e., expense patterns for a 3-month period—are obtained for food and other selected items, accounting for an additional 20 percent to 25 percent of total household expenditures.

In the diary component of the Consumer Expenditure survey, consumers are asked to maintain a complete record of expenses for two consecutive one-week periods. The Consumer Expenditure diary survey was designed to obtain detailed data on frequently purchased small items, including food and beverages (both at home and in eating places), tobacco, housekeeping supplies, nonprescription drugs, and personal care products and services. Respondents are less likely to recall such items over long periods. Integrating data from the interview and diary surveys thus provides a complete accounting of expenditures and income.

Both the interview and diary surveys collect data on household characteristics and income. Data on household characteristics are used to determine the eligibility of the family for inclusion in the population covered by the Consumer Price Index, to classify families for purposes of analysis, and to adjust for nonresponse by families who do not complete the survey.

---

[3]Much of the material in this section is excerpted from Appendix B of *Consumer Expenditure Survey, 1996-97,* Report 935, Bureau of Labor Statistics, September 1999.

Household demographic characteristics are also used to integrate data from the interview and diary components.

Construction of the CPI Market-Basket System

The BLS prices the CPI market basket and produces the monthly CPI index using a complex, multistage sampling process. The first stage involves the selection of urban areas that will constitute the CPI geographic sample. Because the CPI market basket is constructed using data from the Consumer Expenditure survey, the geographic areas selected for the CPI for All Urban Areas are also used in the Consumer Expenditure survey. Once selected, the CPI geographic sample is fixed for 10 years until new census data become available. Using the information supplied by families in the Consumer Expenditure surveys, the BLS constructs the CPI market basket by partitioning the set of all consumer goods and services into a hierarchy of increasingly detailed categories, referred to as the CPI item structure. Each item category is assigned an expenditure weight, or importance, based on its share of total family expenditures. One can ultimately view the CPI market basket as a set of item categories and associated expenditure weights.

Updating and Improving the CPI Market Basket

Because of the many important uses of the monthly CPI, there is great interest in ensuring that the CPI market basket accurately reflects changes in consumption over time. Each decade, data from the U.S. census of population and housing are used to update the CPI process in three key respects: (1) redesigning the national geographic sample to reflect shifts in population; (2) revising the CPI item structure to represent current consumption patterns; and (3) modifying the expenditure weights to reflect changes in the item structure as well as reallocation of the family budget.

CONCLUSIONS AND RECOMMENDATIONS

It is apparent from the discussion in this chapter that all decisions about the configuration and features of the NAEP market basket involve tradeoffs. Some methods for configuring the market basket would result in simpler procedures than others but would not support the desired inferences. Other methods would yield more generalizable results but at the expense of simplicity. The simplest methods would use parallel short forms for data collection and observed scores for reporting, but this configuration may not yield forms and scores generalizable to the larger content domain. The most generalizable results would be based on a system of arbitrary forms with performance reported as the estimated proficiency score (i.e., latent trait estimates), as is currently done with NAEP. However, this is also one of the most complex configurations.

If NAEP's sponsors decide to proceed with designing a market basket, decision making about its configuration should be based on a clear articulation of the purposes and objectives for the market basket. The needs the market basket will serve and the intended uses should guide decisions about its features.

> **RECOMMENDATION 4-1: All decisions about the configuration of the NAEP market basket will involve tradeoffs. Some methods for configuring the market basket would result in simpler procedures than others but would not support the desired inferences. Other methods would yield more generalizable results but at the expense of simplicity. If the decision is made to proceed with designing a NAEP market basket, its configuration should be based on a clear articulation of the purposes and objectives for the market basket.**

CPI Market Basket Versus A NAEP Index: Parallels and Contrasts

The task of building an educational parallel to the CPI is formidable and appears to differ conceptually from the current NAEP market-basket development activities. It is unknown how well the final market-basket instrument, in whatever format, will serve its major goal of better informing the American public regarding the educational accomplishments of its students. The eventual attainment of this goal must begin with a definition of educational accomplishments along with serious consideration of the psychometric properties of the instruments that must be in place to support the desired score inferences.

In considering the proposals to develop and report a summary measure from the existing NAEP frameworks, the committee realized that the proposals for the NAEP market basket differ fundamentally from purpose and construction of the CPI market basket. Although the NAEP frameworks are developed by committees of experts familiar with school-level curricula, they are not descriptive; that is, they are not based on surveys of what schools actually teach.

Implementing a market-basket approach for NAEP, analogous to that used by the CPI, would thus necessitate major operational changes. The design that would most directly parallel that of the CPI would call for surveying classrooms to determine the content and skills currently being taught to students. This is analogous to surveying households to find out what consumers are buying. In the CPI context, the household surveys create a market basket of goods. In the NAEP context, the surveys would lead to a "market basket" of instructional content that would need to reflect regional differences in what is taught. Test forms would be constructed to represent this instructional content and administered to evaluate students' mastery of the material. The resulting scores would indicate how much students know about the currently taught subject matter. Hence, if the NAEP market basket were constructed to parallel the CPI market basket, it would include items representing what survey data show is currently taught in classrooms.

> **CONCLUSION 4-1: Use of the term "market basket" is misleading, because (1) the NAEP frameworks reflect the aspirations of policy makers and educators and are not purely descriptive in nature and (2) the current operational features of NAEP differ fundamentally from the data collection processes used in producing the CPI.**

> **RECOMMENDATION 4-2: In describing the various proposals for reporting a summary measure from the existing NAEP frameworks, NAEP's sponsors should refrain from using the term "market basket" because of inaccuracies in the implied analogy with the CPI.**

> **RECOMMENDATION 4-3: If, given the issues raised about market-basket reporting, NAEP's sponsors wish to pursue the development of this concept, they should consider developing an educational index that possesses characteristics analogous to those of the Consumer Price Index: (1) is descriptive rather than reflecting policy makers' and educators' aspirations; (2) is reflective of regional differences in educational programs; and (3) is updated regularly to incorporate changes in curriculum.**

5
Changed NAEP:
Use of a Short-Form Version of NAEP

As currently configured, NAEP employs a matrix sampling method for administering items to students (see Chapter 2) but does not include the option for administering a fixed test form to large numbers of individuals (Allen, Carlson, & Zelenak, 1998). Implementing such an option will require major changes to the way NAEP test forms are constructed and NAEP results are reported. Such changes are certainly within the realm of possibilities, however. NAGB has active working groups (National Assessment Governing Board, 1999c; National Assessment Governing Board, 2000a) looking into alternate delivery and reporting models for NAEP, and the short form and market-basket concepts originated from the activities of those groups.

This chapter deals explicitly with the short form and addresses the questions: (1) What role might a short form play in providing market-basket results; and (2) How might the short form be used? The chapter begins with a discussion of NAGB's policy and plans for the short form, which is followed by a description of the ways states and districts might use the short forms based on comments from participants in the committee's workshop on market-basket reporting. The chapter continues with a review of the pilot study of short forms and ends with discussion of ways to construct short forms.

STUDY APPROACH

During the course of the study, we reviewed policy statements address-ing the short form (National Assessment Governing Board, 1996; National Assessment Governing Board, 1999a; National Assessment Governing Board, 1999b; Forsyth et al., 1996) and information on the ETS year 2000 pilot study on market-basket reporting (Mazzeo, 2000). We asked Patricia Kenny, co-director of the National Council of Teachers of Mathematics (NCTM) NAEP Interpretive Reports Project, to review the two short forms developed for the pilot study. We also focused specifically on the short form during our workshop on market-basket reporting and asked participants to discuss their interest in and potential uses for the short form of NAEP (see Chapter 4 for additional details on the workshop).

WHAT ARE NAEP SHORT FORMS AND HOW MIGHT THEY BE USED?

Policy for the NAEP Short Form

In the most recent redesign policy, the short form is cited as a mecha-nism for simplifying NAEP design, specifically (National Assessment Gov-erning Board, 1999a:7):

> Plans for the short-form of the National Assessment, using a single test book-let, are being implemented. The purpose of the short-form test is to enable faster, more understandable initial reporting of results and, possibly, for states to have access to test instruments allowing them to obtain NAEP assessment results in years in which NAEP assessments are not scheduled in particular subjects.

To guide policy and decision making on the measurement issues per-taining to the short forms, NAGB adopted the following principles (National Assessment Governing Board, 1999b):

> **Principle 1:** The NAEP short form shall not violate the Congressional prohi-bition to produce, report, or maintain individual examinee scores.
> **Principle 2:** The Board shall decide which grades and subjects shall be as-sessed using a short form.
> **Principle 3:** Development costs, including item development, field testing, scoring, scaling, and linking shall be borne by the NAEP program. The costs associated with use, including administration, scoring, analysis, and report-ing shall be borne by the user.
> **Principle 4:** NAEP short forms intended for actual administration should

represent the content of corresponding NAEP assessment frameworks as fully as possible. Any departure from this principle must be approved by the Board.

Principle 5: Since it is desirable to report the results of the short form using the achievement levels, the content achievement level descriptions should be considered during the development of the short form.

Principle 6: All versions of the short form should be linked to the extent possible using technically sound statistical procedures.

The National Assessment Governing Board's Vision and Uses for the Short Form

At the committee's workshop on market-basket reporting, Roy Truby, executive director of NAGB, explained the concept of the NAEP short form, describing it as a short, administrable test representative of the content domain tested on NAEP (Truby, 2000). Results on the short form could be summarized using a percent correct metric. The short form could provide additional data collection opportunities that are not part of the standard NAEP schedule, such as testing in off years or in other subjects not assessed at the state level. Truby described how some people envision using a short form:

> If short forms were developed and kept secure, they could provide flexibility to states and any jurisdiction below the state level that were interested in using NAEP for surveying student achievement in subjects, grades, and times that were not part of the regular state-NAEP schedule. Once developed, such market-basket forms should be faster and less expensive to administer, score, and report than the standard NAEP, and could provide score distributions without the complex statistical methods on which NAEP now relies. This might help states and others link their own assessments to NAEP, which is another important objective of the Board's redesign policy.

Truby noted that the details associated with these components of the market-basket concept have not yet been thoroughly investigated. Based on the pilot study findings (see Mazzeo, 2000), NAGB might pursue similar studies in other content areas and grades.

Workshop Participants' Visions and Uses for the Short Form

Some school administrators and directors of assessment were attracted to the concept of the short form as a means for obtaining benchmarking data. They envisioned the short form as a test that could be administered to an entire cohort of students (e.g., all fourth grade students in a school or in a district); short form results could be quickly derived and aggregated to the appropriate levels (i.e., school or district level). Under this vision for the short form, summaries of short-form results could be compared to those for national NAEP to provide schools and districts with information on how their students' achievement compared with national results. Participants believed that this information would be uniquely useful in assessing students' strengths and weaknesses and in setting goals for improving student achievement.

Some school administrators and assessment directors also envisioned the short form as a set of questions that could be embedded into current assessments as a mechanism for "linking" results from current assessments to NAEP. Under this vision, the set of questions could be administered in conjunction with other state or local assessments. Short form results could be used to enable comparisons between state and local assessment and main NAEP. It is important to point out that the issues associated with establishing linkages between NAEP and state and local assessments were previously addressed by two other NRC committees (National Research Council, 1999a; National Research Council, 1999d), who cited numerous problems with such practices.

Curriculum specialists saw the short form as a way to gather additional information about what is tested on NAEP and how it compares to their instructional programs. The released short form could permit educators and policy makers to have first-hand access to the material included on the test. Their review of the released material could promote discussions about what is tested and how it compares with the skills and material covered by their own curriculum. The secure short form would yield data that could further these discussions. Educators could examine student data and evaluate performance in relation to their local practices. They could engage in discussions about their curricula, instructional practices, and sequencing of instructional material, and could contemplate changes that might be needed.

Participants also liked the idea of having a NAEP test to administer in "off-years" from regular NAEP administrations. Because NAEP does not currently administer every subject to every grade every year, workshop participants believed the short form could help fill the "gaps." The short form could be given every year thereby enabling the compilation of yearly trend data. These uses for the short forms are discussed in greater detail in the workshop summary (National Research Council, 2000).

Workshop Participants' Concerns About the Short Forms

Some workshop speakers challenged the premises behind the various uses for the short form. Several questioned how comparable scores on the short forms would be to results from NAEP. As described in Chapter 2, NAEP uses complex procedures for deriving score estimates (including the conditioning and plausible values methodologies). If short form results were provided quickly and without the complex statistical methods, results from the short form would not be conditioned; hence short form results would not be comparable to the regular NAEP-scale results.

Comparisons between short form results and state or local assessment results also might not yield the type of information desired. State and local assessments are part of an overall program in which curricula, instruction, and assessments are aligned. However, alignment may not extend to the NAEP frameworks, and the short form might test areas not covered by the curriculum. While it might be enlightening to compare NAEP's coverage with local curricula, testing students on material they have not been taught presents problems for interpreting the results.

Student motivation would also factor into performance on the short form. State and local assessments tend to be higher stakes exams that carry consequences. At present, NAEP is not a high-stakes test. Administration of the short form as part of a high-stakes assessment would change the context in ways that could affect the comparability between results on the short form and the regular NAEP results.

The prohibition against individual results was also cited as problematic. The short form could be administered in a manner closely resembling other testing—testing that results in individual score reports. Although individual results would be generated initially from the short form, they would need to be aggregated for reporting purposes. Participants felt that this prohibition would be difficult to explain. These concerns about the short form are discussed in detail in the workshop summary (National Research Council, 2000).

Review of the Pilot Short Forms

As explained in Chapter 4, ETS prepared two fourth grade mathematics short forms as part of the year 2000 pilot study. One of the two pilot short forms contains 31 items and the other 33. These items were intended to represent NAEP's existing fourth grade mathematics item pools. During the workshop, Bock (2000) estimated that the reliability of the short form would be likely to fall in the low .80 range. While this might be considered acceptable, the more pertinent concern for the short form is not reliability but generalizability. That is, would performance on the short-form support inferences about performance on the larger domain of mathematics? For the workshop, the committee asked Patricia Kenney to consider the feasibility of creating short forms for fourth grade mathematics and the extent to which the developed short forms were representative of what NAEP tests.

Kenney reported that the short forms appeared to represent the general content strands and the item types in the frameworks. However, she questioned whether the forms covered the full range of cognitive processes the framework describes, as well as all of the 56 topics and subtopics covered by the NAEP frameworks. Kenney questioned the extent to which approximately 30 items would be able to adequately represent the frameworks at the topic or subtopic level (Kenney, 2000). Additionally, NAEP items can be administered at more than one grade level. Because NAEP results are not reported at the student level, there is no disadvantage for assessing students on topics that they may not have studied. The problem with these "grade overlap" items, however, is that they might become misinterpreted as NAEP grade-appropriate expectations. Considering the uses cited above for the short forms, Kenney was concerned about how these grade overlap items would be regarded (Kenney, 2000).

THE DESIRED CHARACTERISTICS OF A SHORT FORM

Given the alternative visions and uses described above, we can now consider options for constructing and implementing short form NAEP. NAGB policy (National Assessment Governing Board, 1999b) states that "NAEP short forms intended for actual administration should represent the content of corresponding NAEP assessment frameworks as fully as possible" (Principle 4). This statement implies that NAGB's intent is to produce short forms that are samples of the domain represented by the framework. While it does not seem to be the intent to represent the current NAEP item pool, or to create scales, the short form needs to be capable of providing estimates of the true score distribution that is the target for full NAEP. That distribution is needed to support policy Principle 5, "Since it is desirable to report the results of the short form using the achievement levels, the content achievement level descriptions should be considered during the development of the short form." Reporting results according to the achievement levels requires an accurate estimation of the proficiency distribution. Estimation of the distribution requires the specification of a scale.

NAGB policy does not provide any further guidance about the desired technical characteristics for the short form. While the generality of policy statements is appropriate so that developers are not limited in the approaches they consider for putting policy into practice, the lack of detail allows a variety of interpretations. For example, the state and district test directors imagine a short form of 10 to 15 items that can be embedded in their tests as anchors to link their tests to the NAEP scale (O'Reilly, 2000). The ETS-produced pilot versions contain 31 and 33 items (Mazzeo, 2000)—twice the length imagined by the test directors. Since the ETS pilot short form was limited by other constraints, additional conceptions would also be feasible.

The NAGB materials (National Assessment Governing Board, 1999b) and the discussions at the workshop (National Research Council, 2000) imply the following specifications for the short form.

1. The short form should represent the NAEP framework.
2. The short form should be at least somewhat consistent with the achievement level descriptions.
3. It should be possible to aggregate the data from the short forms to provide good estimates of mean performance for subgroups of the student population.
4. It should be possible to estimate the proportion above the achievement level cutscores. This implies that the short form can support estimation of the distribution of scores on the NAEP scale.
5. It should be possible to compare results from alternate forms of short forms for a curriculum area, which implies that the short forms are to be put on a common score scale, perhaps through an equating process.
6. Some would like to use the short form as an anchor test for connecting other testing programs to the NAEP reporting scale. This use is not addressed by the policy for the short form.

These specifications present a challenging development task because the short form will necessarily have different psychometric characteristics than the full set of current NAEP items or any one of the NAEP booklets. Successful accomplishment of this development task depends on the degree to which each requirement must be met. For example, if the level of accuracy of a mean estimate from the short form does not have to be as great as that for the full NAEP, then requirement 3 can probably be met. However, if the level of accuracy of the mean estimates must be the same as for full NAEP, then the design of the short form and its administration plan will be very challenging. To assist NAEP's sponsors with these difficult issues, we consider them next.

MEETING THE DESIRED SPECIFICATIONS FOR THE SHORT FORMS

Representing the Frameworks

The first requirement is that the short form should represent the NAEP framework. However, "represent" is open to multiple interpretations. One interpretation is a formal statistical sampling from a population. If every item in the domain had an equal chance of being sampled, the resulting sample would represent the entire population. The short form could then either represent the domain (i.e., the framework) or the current NAEP pool. These are not synonymous because the current NAEP pool may not "represent" the NAEP framework in any statistical sense; that is, the items in the NAEP pool are not a random sample from the domain.

A short form could be constructed to "represent" the current NAEP pool in a statistical sense by randomly sampling items from that pool. Such a sample might not include items from every content specification category, but they would be an unbiased statistical sample and would therefore represent the larger number of items.

A more general interpretation of "represent" might be that the short form provides "examples" of the types of tasks required by NAEP. Under this interpretation, the NAEP item pool would be considered to represent the framework, and any set of items that assesses the skills listed in the framework would represent the framework by example. Because the framework is very broad, it would be impossible to present sample items for every type of skill and knowledge in the framework. Thus for practical reasons, the short form's representation of the framework must be incomplete, and the short form would represent the framework less well than the full NAEP pool represented the framework.

An even looser interpretation of "represent" could be that the items on a short form provide selected examples of the kinds of items developed from the framework. The items in the NAEP pool could be sorted according to the skills required by the achievement level descriptions to help meet requirement 2. While these sortings would not be perfectly reliable, they could support a loose definition of representation. Either a stratified sampling of 30 items could be drawn from that pool, or a carefully reasoned sample could be selected to produce a descriptive example of the pool. If the current NAEP items cannot be used, new items could be produced that measure skills consistent with the frameworks document. All of these options meet a loose definition of "represent."

Approaches to Constructing Short Forms

The *Standards for Educational and Psychological Tests* (American Educational Research Association, American Psychological Association, & National Council on Measurement in Education, 1999) present guidelines to be followed in constructing a short form version of a longer test. Specifically, Standard 3.16 states:

> If a short form of a test is prepared, for example, by reducing the number of items on the original test or organizing portions of a test into a separate form, the specifications of the short form should be as similar as possible to those of the original test. The procedure for reduction of items should be documented.

Given these guidelines, we describe two procedures that could be used to develop short forms.

Domain Sampling Approach

Given that the goal of NAEP is to assess the knowledge and skills of fourth, eighth, and twelfth grade students in the areas defined by the frameworks, the measurement model that seems most appropriate to this task is domain sampling (Nunnally, 1967:175). If a domain sampling approach were to be used, the NAEP framework would define the domain, and the goal of test development would be to produce an instrument that contains tasks that are an appropriate sample from that domain. Ideally, the framework would be translated into specifications that clearly delimit the types of items included in the domain.

With this approach, developers would produce many items that represented the domain, and forms would be developed by sampling from the set of items. For the purposes of the present discussion, the full set of all NAEP items included in all forms given to students during an operational NAEP administration will be considered the long form. It cannot be considered a long form in the usual sense, because no student would take all of the items. However, the "long form" would define the score scale for reporting NAEP results. The short form would simply be a test containing fewer items than the long form.

Under a domain sampling approach, a short form of NAEP could be developed by selecting a smaller sample of items than for the long form. This process for creating a short form would address Standard 3.16 because the specifications for the domain are the same for both the short and long form. If formal statistical sampling procedures were used, both the long form and the short form would represent the full domain but to different degrees of accuracy.

The NAEP item and form development process has not been as formal as the domain sampling model. A large pool of items has been produced to match the content and cognitive skills described in each framework document, but the items that have been produced were not intended to be a statistically representative sample from the domain (Allen, Carlson, & Zelenak, 1998). The framework documents do not define clear boundaries for the domain (Forsyth, 1991), and no criteria are given for determining whether or not an item is a part of the domain. At best, the items in a set of NAEP booklets for a content area can be considered to be a sample from the domain, but a sample with unknown statistical properties.

Hence, construction of a short form becomes more challenging than merely taking a statistical sample from a well-defined pool of items. Because the NAEP forms are an idiosyncratic sample from the domain, the best approach from a domain sampling perspective is to select a sample of items from the current set of items. The resulting sample would be representative of the items on a current set of NAEP forms, but would not necessarily be representative of the full domain. The stratified random sampling plan could be used to make sure that important content strands are proportionally represented.

Scale Construction Approach

An alternative procedure might be based on the trait estimation approach commonly used in psychology (McDonald, 1999), which defines a hypothetical construct and then selects test items estimated to be highly correlated with the construct. While the resulting set of items defines a scale for the construct, there is no intention to define a domain of content or to sample from the domain. The test development process is considered effective as long as the set of items rank orders individuals on the scale for the hypothetical construct.

Employing this approach with NAEP would imply that NAEP's purpose is to place students along one or more continua based on their responses to the test items. The items would be selected to define scales rather than to represent the domain. To be consistent with the requirements of Standard 3.16, the short form would have to define the same scales as the full NAEP.

Precision of Measurement

Either approach to developing a short form would result in a test with different measurement properties than a "long" form. For instance, scores from the short form will have less precision of measurement than a test consisting of the full set of current NAEP items. The comment to Standard 3.16 addresses the differences in measurement properties and calls for their documentation, saying:

> The extent to which the specifications of the short form differ from those of the original test, and the implications of such differences for interpreting the scores derived from the short form, should be documented.

One clear difference between the short form and the long form is that scores from the short form will have a different reliability and standard error structure[1] than those from the full NAEP pool even though the short form and full NAEP provide samples from the same domain of content (National Research Council, 2000).

If the domain sampling approach is used, the short form will result in greater sampling error than full NAEP because a smaller sample is taken from the content domain. Although both sets of items (test forms) would represent the domain, and both would measure the same constructs, the smaller sample would have larger estimation error.

---

[1]Standard error structure refers to the pattern of conditional standard errors of measurement at different points on the reporting score scale. Because of the different lengths of the two forms, the conditional standard errors will certainly not be the same at every point on the score scale.

Under the scale formation approach, the content framework determines the number of scales that need to be considered. For example, NAEP Mathematics reports scores that are weighted composites of five scales (National Assessment Governing Board, 2000) that are combined using weights to form a composite that is used for reporting. When the test is shortened, the number of scales would remain the same, but fewer items would be used to define the scales. Because the scale of measurement for the short form would be defined with less fine gradations than defined by the full set of items, scores would be estimated with less precision of measurement.

Discussions of the relative standard error of measurement for the short form and the full NAEP must be carefully considered. In the matrix sampling design used by NAEP, the standard error of measurement for a student is large for long form NAEP—possibly larger than the standard error of measurement for a hypothetical short form. However, estimates of population parameters, such as the population mean and standard deviation, are based on the full set of items and the full sample of students, and they use collateral background information to "condition" the estimation process (see Chapter 2). Consequently, the estimation of population parameters should be much more precise for full NAEP than for a short form even though the short form might yield smaller measurement error for a student's score if individual scores were permitted to be generated for NAEP.

Technical Requirements for a Short Form

The technical requirements for a short form are very challenging. Requirements 3 and 4 suggest that the short form allow estimation of means and percentages of distributions on the NAEP scale. This implies that the short form would produce scores on the same composite of skills as the full NAEP pool. This is also required by Standard 3.16. Producing a short form that will result in scores that fulfill the statistical requirements will require careful matching of content and statistical characteristics of the items on the short form to the NAEP item pool. This can best be done using multidimensional procedures to select items that create the desired composite score and a score distribution that is similar to that from the full NAEP sample. In theory, this could be accomplished using the full set of tools available from IRT and computerized test assembly methodologies. Even with those tools, however, the test assembly process will be difficult, and it will be necessary to confirm that the desired composite of abilities is assessed.

CONCLUSIONS AND RECOMMENDATIONS

The committee's review of the materials on the short form concept indicates that NAGB and potential consumers of short form results have varying conceptions of the short form. Some (McConachie, 2000; O'Reilly, 2000) believe the short form should function as an anchor test that can be used to link various types of assessments to NAEP so the results can be reported on the NAEP score scale. Others (Mazzeo, 2000; Truby, 2000) view the short form as a mechanism for implementing market-basket reporting or as a way of facilitating district-level reporting and providing more responsive reporting of NAEP results (O'Reilly, 2000; Truby, 2000). These differing views about the short form make it difficult for the committee to make specific recommendations because so many details have yet to be decided. Nevertheless, the conception of many workshop participants that the short form could be used as an anchor to put state assessment results on the NAEP scale is not likely to be tenable. The difficulties associated with attempts to achieve such links among assessments have been documented in previous reports by other NRC committees (National Research Council, 1999a; National Research Council, 1999d).

CONCLUSION 5-1. Thus far, the NAEP short form has been defined by general NAGB policy, but it has not been developed in sufficient technical and practical detail that potential users can react to a firm proposal. Instead, users are projecting into the general idea their own desired characteristics for the short form, such as an anchor for linking scales. Some of their ideas and desires for the short form have already been determined to be problematic. It will not be possible for a short form design to support all uses described by workshop participants.

The most positive result that can be expected from attempts at short form construction is that the short form is shown to measure the same composite of skills and knowledge as the full NAEP pool and that the distribution of statistical item characteristics is such that the shape of the estimated score distribution will be similar, though not identical, to that for current NAEP. The distribution will probably not be exactly the same because of differences in the error distribution that result from using a shorter test. The practical result is that the mean scores estimated from the short form will probably have larger standard errors than those from the full NAEP and that the estimates of proportions above the achievement level cutscores will also contain more error. The results from the short form will probably look different than those from full NAEP, even if exactly the same students took both types of tests. The differences in error will add "noise" to the results of the two types of tests in different ways.

Comparisons of short form and full NAEP results will not be easy, even for technically sophisticated consumers. The fact that the two sets of results are not directly comparable does not mean that the short form might not be useful. It does mean, however, that the differences in interpretation must be made clear to avoid confusion. One way would be to use different score scales and to report short form scores as estimates of the proportion of the full NAEP pool that students would get correct rather than scores on the NAEP score scale. In this case, the error in estimates could be indicated with error bars or other reporting methods. Use of different score scales would preclude making direct comparisons, but the short form may still have value as a more frequent monitor of student capabilities. However, it is worth restating here that, to many workshop participants, being able to make comparisons with main NAEP was one of the more appealing features of the short form.

> **CONCLUSION 5-2: The method selected for producing a short form will likely result in a test that has a different reliability (error structure) than the full NAEP, resulting in different estimates of the score distribution than the full NAEP. As a result, the short form will likely give different numerical results than the full NAEP, even if the samples of students were identical.**

> **RECOMMENDATION 5-1: Before attempting to use a short form version of NAEP to estimate results on the current NAEP scale, the differences in the psychometric characteristics of the scores from the short form and current NAEP should be carefully investigated.**

> **RECOMMENDATION 5-2: Before proceeding with the short form, it should be determined whether it is possible to obtain estimates of NAEP score distributions from the short form**

that will provide estimates of proportions above achievement levels and means for subgroups of the examinee population that are of similar accuracy to those from current NAEP.

RECOMMENDATION 5-3: If the decision is made to proceed with the short form, methods should be developed for reporting performance on the short form in a way that is meaningful and not misleading given the differences in quality of estimates for current NAEP and the short form.

6
Designing Reports of District-Level and Market-Basket NAEP Results

The goal of NAEP is to inform our society about the status of educational achievement in the United States and, more recently, in specific states. Currently, policy makers are considering if NAEP data gathered from still smaller geopolitical units and based on smaller numbers of test items can be used to generate meaningful reports for a variety of constituents. These proposed reporting practices emanate from desires to improve the usefulness and ease of interpretation of NAEP data. Both proposals call for close attention to the format and contents of the new reports.

When NAEP first proposed producing state-level results, a number of concerns were expressed about potential misinterpretation or misuse of the data (Stancavage et al., 1992; Hartka & Stancavage, 1994). With the provision of below-state NAEP results, the potential for reporting/misinterpretation problems is also high. If readers are proud, distressed, or outraged by their statewide results, their reaction to district or hometown results are likely to be even stronger. In addition, the wider variety of education and media professionals providing the public with information about local-level test results is also likely to contribute to potential interpretation problems. These professionals may have a greater variety of positions to promote as well as more varied levels of statistical sophistication. In short, consideration of effective reporting formats may become more urgent.

Even if the proposals for district-level and market-basket reporting do not come to fruition, attention to the way NAEP information is provided would be useful. As described in Chapter 2, the types of NAEP reports are

many and varied. The information serves many purposes for a broad constellation of audiences, including researchers, policy makers, the press, and
the public. These audiences, both the more technical users and the lay
public, look to NAEP to support, refute, or inform their ideas about the
academic accomplishments of students in the United States. The messages
taken from NAEP's data displays can easily influence their perceptions
about the state of education in the United States.

Generally, both technical users and the lay public tend to extract whatever possible from data displays. Unfortunately, the "whatever possible"
often translates to "very little" for at least two reasons. First, readers may
pay very little attention to data reports, feeling that the time required to
decode often arcane reports is not well spent; the data are not worth the
additional effort. Second, even when readers carefully study the displays,
they might misinterpret the data. Even well-intentioned report designs fall
prey to the cognitive and perceptual misinterpretations of the most serious
reader (Monmonier, 1991; Cleveland & McGill, 1984; Tversky & Schiano,
1989).

Earlier chapters of this report have focused on the feasibility and desirability of collecting and reporting such data. This chapter focuses on the
end product—the reports released for public consumption. As part of our
study, the committee hoped to review prototypes of district-level and
market-basket reports. NCES provided an example of a district-level report
that was part of an early draft of technical specifications for below-state
reporting, and Milwaukee shared with us the report they received as part of
their participation in a district-level pilot. These reports were presented as
drafts and examples, not as the definitive formats for district-level reports.
We reviewed one preliminary mock-up of a market-basket report based on
simulated data (Johnson, Laser, & O'Sullivan, 1997). Since ETS is currently designing reports as part of the second year of the year 2000 pilot
project on market-basket reporting, much of the decision making about
market-basket reports has not yet occurred. Given the stage of the work
on district-level and market-basket reporting, we present the following discussion to assist NAEP's sponsors with the design of the reports.

This chapter begins with a review and description of some problems
cited with regard to the presentations of NAEP data. For this review, we
relied on the work of a number of researchers, specifically, Hambleton and
Slater (1995); Wainer (1997); and Jaeger (1998); Wainer, Hambleton, &
Meara (1999); and Hambleton & Meara (2000). The next section pro-

vides commentary on report samples reviewed during the study. The documents reviewed include the following:

1. *Draft Guidelines and Technical Specifications for the Conduct of Assessments Below-State Level NAEP Testing, NCES, August, 1995, Draft*, which included a mock-up of a report for a district (National Center for Education Statistics, 1995).
2. NAEP 1996 Science Report for Milwaukee Public Schools, Grade 8, Findings from a special study of the National Assessment of Educational Progress (Educational Testing Service, 1997b)
3. NAEP 1996 Mathematics Report for Milwaukee Public Schools, Grade 8, Findings from a special study of the National Assessment of Educational Progress (Educational Testing Service, 1997a)
4. Sample market-basket report based on simulated data (Johnson, Lazer, & O'Sullivan, 1997)
5. *NAEP's Year 2000 Market-Basket Study: What Do We Expect to Learn?* (Mazzeo, 2000)

The chapter concludes with additional suggestions for enhancing the accessibility and comprehensibility of NAEP reports. To assist in the design of future reports, we encourage the application of procedures to make the data more useable, including user- and needs-assessment, heuristic evaluation, and actual usability testing. In the appendix to this report, we provide an example of how these techniques might be applied.

CRITIQUES OF NAEP DATA DISPLAYS

To date, a number of concerns with the accessibility and comprehensibility of NAEP reports have been described. The most consistent concerns are discussed below.

High-Level Knowledge of Statistics Is Assumed

Reports assume an inappropriately high level of statistical knowledge for even well-educated lay audiences. There are too many technical terms, symbols, and concepts required to understand the message of even relatively simple data, such as mean test scores as a function of time or location. In interviews assessing policy makers', educational administrators' and media representatives' understanding of NAEP reports, Hambleton and Slater

(1995) reported that 42 percent did not understand the meaning of "statistically significant." Even relatively basic mathematical symbols are the source of some misunderstanding. For example, roughly one-third of those interviewed by Hambleton and Slater did not understand the meaning of the '>' and '<' symbols that were used to indicate a reliable increase or decrease in mean scores.

Information Overload and Report Density

In an attempt to be complete, reports may present too much information, making it difficult for readers to find and extract what they really want to know. Wainer (1997a) described this problem in detail with respect to NAEP tables, but the same arguments would hold for other formats as well. Reports also often contain overly dense displays that readers find daunting. This problem deals with readers' perceptions of ease of access. Designers of textbooks and other technical documents have learned that reports can be designed to appear more or less difficult to understand just by varying simple report features such as the amount and placement of "white space" on the page. In addition to ensuring that reports are easy to understand, care must be taken to make reports *look* easy to understand.

Attempts at Redesign Have Increased "Clutter"

When displays are redesigned for easy access, design devices are sometimes used that undermine this objective through increased clutter or perceptual inaccuracies. That is, designers can go too far in their attempts to make data appear more enticing. A case in point is the use of three-dimensional renderings of data, where line graphs become cliffs, and pie charts become floating discs. Three-dimensional renderings are inherently ambiguous when the information to be extracted involves relative size judgments of parts, such as, the relative heights of two bars in a three-dimensional bar graph. So, while attempts should be focused on making data reports appear more accessible, concurrent design reviews should ensure that comprehensibility is not compromised.

Unnecessary Mental Arithmetic Is Required

Reports sometimes require readers to perform unnecessary mental steps, including unreliable mental arithmetic, to derive information most relevant to them. For example, change scores across NAEP administrations may be as important to most readers as the absolute mean scores at each individual administration. Mistakes in mental arithmetic can easily lead to incorrect interpretations, even among readers who understand the meaning of the presented data.

Graphics Are Infrequently Used

Reports do not make enough use of graphical alternatives to textual and tabular formats. Associated with both the actual and perceived complexity issues noted above, reports use vast tables of numbers more frequently than necessary. Some researchers (e.g., Wainer, 1997a; Wainer et al., 1999) argue that, in many cases, graphical displays are more appropriate than tables. In an experimental study comparing redesigned NAEP data displays, many of which were graphs, with traditional NAEP displays consisting primarily of tables, Wainer demonstrated that the graphical formats promote more rapid and accurate interpretations (Wainer et al., 1999).

> **CONCLUSION 6-1: Enhancements to the design of NAEP reports that allow for communication to a broader audience are a way to increase the utility of these tests, independent of changes to the methods used to collect and analyze the actual data. The data currently available can be made more accessible, comprehensible, and relevant.**

REVIEW OF SAMPLE DISTRICT-LEVEL AND MARKET-BASKET REPORTS

District-Level Reports

NCES' *Specifications for Below-state Reporting* (National Center for Education Statistics, 1995), still considered a draft document, included a report summarizing results for one of the "naturally occurring" districts. This report was in tabular format and included means, standard deviations, quartiles, and percents at or above each achievement level. Data were reported for test takers grouped by gender, ethnicity, parents' educational level, type of location, Title I participation, and eligibility status in the school lunch program. Very basic (and somewhat cryptic) interpretive information described the grouping categories and the statistics reported.

The reports prepared for the Milwaukee Public School system consisted entirely of tables accompanied by detailed explanatory text. To enable comparisons, the tables included results for Milwaukee, Wisconsin, and the United States. The report contained numerous two-way tables that presented mean scaled scores for test takers grouped by demographic (e.g., gender, ethnicity, parental education), school environment (e.g., parental support, absenteeism, availability of classroom resources), and classroom characteristics (e.g., amount of homework assigned, availability of computers). Appendices provided guidance on grouping categories and on the reported statistics.

Critique of District-Level Reports

To begin our review, we compared the sample district-level reports, particularly those prepared for Milwaukee, with some of the standard NAEP reports. Although the district-level efforts attempted to make the reports more readable, while limiting misinterpretations, there is still substantial room for improvement.

The most salient deficiency in both reports is the proliferation of tables. Much of the data could be relayed succinctly in graphical form, yet none were used. If we were allowed to make only one suggestion about NAEP reporting, it would be to use graphical rather than tabular formats whenever feasible, even when displaying relatively few data values (Carswell & Ramzy, 1997).

The use of graphical formats will help address many of the other problems associated with previous NAEP reports, including information overload and readers' perceptions that the reports are difficult to read. One of the important ways that graphs can reduce overload is by showing relations among display elements, called "emergent features," to allow the reader to draw conclusions without having to hold and manipulate numerical information in their working memory (Bennet & Flach, 1992). For example, a graph with three lines could be used to portray the trends in the relationships between NAEP scale scores and the amount of daily homework students complete for the United States, Wisconsin, and Milwaukee. One line would show the relationship of homework and NAEP scores for the city, another line for the state, and a third for the nation. The direction of the slopes of the lines, and the relationships among the lines (for example, fanning out vs. parallel) can be recognized very rapidly. These emergent features can be used to evaluate relationships among the data for different groups. For example, the relationships between amount of homework assigned and NAEP performance can readily be compared for Milwaukee versus Wisconsin students and versus the nation.

The amount of information presented in individual data displays is a concern for the samples in the below-state technical specifications. The tables reporting achievement-level percentages include seven columns which, based on current knowledge about working memory constraints, is probably about three columns too many. It will be difficult for people to read the table and keep track of which column they are reading while moving down the page, at least without resorting to annoying and error-prone visual scanning to reread the column headings.

Although the Milwaukee report limited most of its tables to between three and five columns, the actual range was from two to seven. While this streamlining aids the readability of individual tables, it adds to the size of the overall report and may make it difficult for some readers to find specific information spread over multiple tables and pages. This potential problem points to the importance of ascertaining users' information needs and priorities during the early stages of report design. For example, if the homework and test score relationships are of greater interest than the relationship between calculator use and test scores, then the homework table should be given priority of position in the report. Determination of the information to be combined in a single display should be based on the types of questions readers tend to ask of the data. Again, it should be noted that the use of graphs rather than tables may allow more variables to be combined in a single display without overloading the reader.

Finally, the language of the reports we reviewed still overestimates the statistical expertise of its audience. For example, in the below-state report specifications, column headings included "n," "cv," and "< basic." Recall that Hambleton and Slater (1995) found that only about one-third of their subjects understood the use of "<" and ">" symbols. The "cv" is likely to be beyond the grasp of most readers, and the "n," though possibly familiar to undergraduates enrolled in a statistics course, is probably a vague memory, at best, for most people. The Milwaukee reports avoided many of these problems by reporting mainly percentages and average-scale scores. However, they did report scale scores by selected percentiles (percent at each quartile), which may not be widely understood.

The Milwaukee reports also provided brief textual interpretations directly above each table. Some interpretations were provided to ensure that readers did not focus too heavily on small, statistically unreliable differences; other interpretations were simply overviews of table content. In general, these brief text inserts are likely to be useful to people searching for specific kinds of information or who may be unfamiliar with inferential statistics and associated notations. However, the writers of these inserts must take care in selecting their terminology and in avoiding the specialized statistical usage of terms such as "significant" in describing results.

Market-Basket Reports

Work on designing market-basket reports is still in its earliest stage. As part of market-basket preliminary research, Johnson and colleagues (1997) provided a sample report based on simulated data. Reactions to this report were obtained during the committee's workshop on market-basket reporting. The mock-up appears below.

Table 6-1 displays percent correct results for test takers in fourth, eighth and twelfth grades. Column 2 presents the overall average percent correct for test takers in each grade. Column 3 shows the percent correct scores for each achievement-level category associated with the minimum score cutpoint for the category. For example, the cutpoint for the fourth-grade advanced category would be associated with a score of 80 percent correct. A score of 33 percent correct would represent performance at the cutpoint for twelfth-grade's basic category.

TABLE 6-1   Example of Market-Basket Results*

(1) Grade	(2) Average Percent Correct Score[†]	(3) Cut Points by Achievement Level		
		Advanced	Proficient	Basic
4	41%	80%	58%	34%
8	42%	73%	55%	37%
12	40%	75%	57%	33%

*Data in Table 6-1 are based on simulations from the full NAEP assessment; results for a market basket might differ depending on its composition.

[†]In terms of total possible points

Comments on this report were mixed, especially given that it was presented as a mock-up and not as a prototype for market-basket reporting. The primary concerns related to substantive issues, specifically the percent correct scores that would be associated with the achievement level descriptors (e.g., 55 percent correct would represent a proficient level). Given this concern, it would be essential to provide explanatory text documenting the meaning of the various achievement level descriptors.

Further design of market-basket reports is an ongoing part of ETS's pilot study. The year 2000 study is expected to yield two type of reports: (1) a research report intended for technical audiences that examines test development and data analytic issues associated with the implementation of market-basket reporting, and (2) a report intended for general audiences. According to Mazzeo (2000), some of the features being explored include

- National and state-level NAEP results (average scores and achievement level percentages) expressed in a market-basket metric (e.g. percent correct). Such results could be confined to "total-group" scores or could be extended to include national and state results by gender, race/ethnicity, parental education, and other standard NAEP reporting groups.
- All, or a sample, of the items that make up the short form as well as performance data. The text of the items, scoring rubrics, and sample student responses might also be provided.
- A format and writing style appropriate for a general public audience.
- Electronic reporting.   .

Pilot study plans call for focus groups to be conducted during the second year to obtain feedback on the report designs. Because report design is in the early development stage and actual prototypic reports are unavailable, we next discuss methods for designing reports to assist NAEP's sponsors with this process.

TOWARD COMPREHENSIBLE AND ACCESSIBLE DISTRICT-LEVEL AND MARKET-BASKET REPORTS: THE ARGUMENT FOR FORMAL USABILITY AUDITS

Current Practice

NCES and NAGB have recognized the need for more attention to the public "face" of NAEP reports, funding research on readers' responses to and understanding of current reports (Jaeger, 1998; Hambleton & Meara, 2000). However, the design reviews and modifications necessary to address the comprehensibility and accessibility issues raised by this research remain fairly informal and unsystematic.

NAGB has encouraged NCES to redirect NAEP reports to the general public and away from more technical audiences (Bourque, personal communication, April 2000). For example, in 1992, NAGB adopted resolutions calling for achievement levels as the primary way of reporting NAEP data, believing that achievement levels are more understandable to the public than the traditional scale scores. In addition, a separate NAGB resolution resulted in the relocation of standard errors—of most interest to the technical community and less so to the public—to the appendices of reports. However, such changes appear to be based on the opinions of board members through NAGB's Dissemination and Reporting Committee, rather than on results from formal usability audits or tests. Although NAEP reports go through NCES departmental reviews and adjudication, it is not current practice to require that a usability expert be a part of the review process.

Suggested Practice

One way to bring the concerns of accessibility and comprehensibility into the design and review process for NAEP reports is through the application of a number of "usability engineering" methods. These methods, which have been applied extensively to consumer product and electronic information design, rely on user-centered feedback and user participation in all phases of development (e.g., Neilsen, 1993; Norman, 1988; Rubin, 1994). Box 6-1 illustrates user-centered design strategies that might be applied to the development and revision of NAEP reports.

After defining the "mission" of the report by incorporating directives, constraints (e.g., costs, time lines), and program requirements, an in-depth

BOX 6-1
Example of design heuristics for evaluating
the usability of data displays

(1) Is the format compatible with the performance criterion selected? If speed of finding and reporting information is more important than absolute accuracy, then graphical or more holistic displays should generally be used. If accuracy of retrieval of precise values is the goal, a tabular display may be required.

(2) Is the structure of the display compatible with the structure of the data? If the data structure has been described prior to choosing a display, then the data structure should determine the format. For example, periodic or cyclic time trends should be presented on a polar plot and linear trends should be presented in the form of a line graph.

(3) Is the perceptual grouping of information compatible with the mental grouping users must perform to extract the information they want and need? Given data from the user needs assessment, are the data values necessary for the most important comparison or integration grouped most strongly (i.e., associated by the greatest number of gestalt grouping principles such as spatial proximity, similarity, connectedness, and enclosure)? Are information values that are rarely combined isolated from one another?

(4) Is the level of numeric detail compatible with the reliability of the data and the needs of the reader? Reporting of decimal places should be reduced to the minimum necessary for the task at hand, as unnecessary precision results in increased reading time and reduced discriminability among numbers (and increased potential for error).

(5) Is data salience compatible with data importance? One of the purposes of some data displays is to direct the reader's attention. Because involuntary shifts of attention are induced by dissimilarity (e.g., a red pie chart in a table filled with blue numbers), make certain that the most dissimilar or incongruent features of the visual array represent information of genuine importance (based on the results of data analysis or on the interests of the users).

(6) Is the data display compatible with working memory limits? Working memory refers to two fundamental phenomena that all humans experience. The first phenomenon is that people retain their immediate thoughts only until other thoughts displace them. New thoughts displace old thoughts because working memory can only hold so much information at a given time. In general, individual displays should include no more than four organizational "objects" that must be used in conjunction (e.g., lines in a graph, columns in a table, or footnote identifier in either type of display). In addition, information to be used in conjunction should be placed together, so that one piece of information does not have to be held in working memory while the reader is looking for the information with which to integrate it.

(7) Are physical properties of the stimuli compatible with our ability to detect, discriminate, and recognize these properties? Does the physical difference in the height of two bars or the slope of two lines exceed the minimum necessary to result in a perceptual just-noticeable-difference (JND)? Are data values that need to be compared presented, where possible, as points along common scales? If points along common scales cannot be used, then are physical dimensions chosen from as near the front of the following as possible—lengths, angles and slopes, volumes, lightness/darkness, and hue? If users must precisely identify a visual element from among a small set of alternatives (e.g., the color of a line that represents the data collected from the far western states rather than the Northeast, Midwest, or South), then different dimensions should be combined redundantly to aid identification and to maximize dissimilarity.

(8) Is the organization of information in the display compatible with spatial metaphors and population stereotypes? Are better scores represented as "higher" scores (e.g., by graphing number correct rather than number of errors)? Are more recent scores reported to the right of earlier scores? Are lines or bars representing more southern geographic regions represented by "warmer" colors?

(9) Is the choice of display format and ornamentation compatible with the users' preferences and biases? Three-dimensional displays should be avoided when showing controversial results, since readers find two-dimensional displays more "trustworthy." Use bar graphs instead of line graphs when readers are likely to be intimidated by statistical displays.

study is needed to identify the target audience and their likely information needs. This is the stage of *user-needs analysis,* an aspect of NAEP design both in terms of test construction and reporting that seems to be somewhat neglected. As we have emphasized elsewhere in this report, we need to know exactly who is interested in district-level and market-basket NAEP data, as well as who is interested in current NAEP data. It will also be necessary to determine users' expectations of what information can be gleaned from the reports; gauge their level of statistical sophistication and experience with educational test data; and elicit information about their experiences, from which guiding metaphors might be derived to aid in translating test data into more understandable concepts.

This information can then be translated into a series of *user requirements.* For example, these requirements should include a list of statistical terms or concepts that the users can be expected to know and a list of terms and concepts likely to be misunderstood. Likewise, the requirements could indicate the minimum reading level of likely users. After gaining information about the users' interests and expectations, a list of "most important questions" can also be generated to inform the selection and ordering of specific data displays in the reports. Knowledge about the users' educational and work histories might provide suggestions for appropriate data metaphors, for example, use of sports statistics rather than economic indices.

With the user requirements identified, report designers can create mock-ups of entire reports and component displays. These mock-ups can use past data or "dummy" data to increase their realism. The mock-ups should then undergo *heuristic evaluations* in which a usability specialist checks the designs against a list of empirically established guidelines for reducing effort, time, and errors in the reading of data displays. Box 6-1 provides one example of a set of such heuristics. However, there are additional guidelines available, such as those described by Jaeger (1998), Pickle and Herrmann for statistical maps (1994), Wainer (1997a) for tables, Spence & Lewandowsky (1989), Kosslyn (1994), and Cleveland (1985), and Gillian, Wickens, Hollands, & Carswell (1998) for graphs.

It is important when choosing and using heuristics for early and rapid usability reviews that care be taken to select scientifically validated heuristics (Herrmann & Pickle, 1996; Kosslyn, 1985; Simkin & Hastie, 1987; Tversky & Schiano, 1989) that are not simply the result of design lore or convention. That is, care should be taken to ensure that the science of human cognition and comprehension informs the art of NAEP reporting.

Suggestions made during the heuristic evaluation can be used to modify the overall report layout or the design of specific displays. At this point, actual usability testing becomes essential. Wainer (1997a) provides an excellent example of this step in the review process. In his study, a sample of potential users answered questions about NAEP data while viewing original and revised data displays. The user-subjects were also timed and probed for their preferences. In the Wainer study, most of the revised displays led to better performance and were preferred. However, there were some exceptions, which should lead to additional design revision or to the reconsideration of the original design for the final report.

Once the reports are produced and distributed, further usability analyses can be made on the actual use of the reports (e.g., citations, requests for copies) and on misuses made of the data (overgeneralizations, errors in interpretation). This information can be integrated into the next user-needs analysis before the next round of NAEP data is published.

Previous critiques of NAEP report design (Jaeger, 1998) have suggested a number of these components in isolation, such as market research to determine user expectations and field testing to review actual usability. Focus groups, like those conducted by Hartka and Stancavage (1994) during evaluations of the Trial State Assessment, provide examples. We suggest that these processes should be applied to the development of the reports issued to NAEP's audience in connection with district-level reporting and the design of market-basket reports. In the appendix to this report, we provide an example of how a usability process might work.

Drawing on Appropriate Imagery

The issue of defining appropriate metaphors to enhance report comprehension is particularly important when considering market-basket style reports. The model that has been used for market-basket reporting is the CPI (Forsyth et al., 1996). For communicating information about fluctuations in the price of consumer goods, the image of an actual market basket is both appropriate and very familiar to consumers. However, a market basket is an odd, even jarring image in the context of educational achievement. Most people probably do not view education as a consumer purchase, nor are they likely to perceive it as an assortment of independent parcels placed in a shopping cart. The question, however, is what metaphor should replace the market basket in representing a composite reporting statistic of NAEP performance? Again, the user-needs analysis is the appropriate forum for determining the most direct or evocative metaphor, be it a "report card," a "GPA," or some sort of educational "batting average."

CONCLUSIONS AND RECOMMENDATIONS

Given the amount of attention that below-state results would be likely to receive, significant time and effort should be devoted to product design. The design of data displays should be carefully reviewed and should evolve through methodical processes to consider the purposes the data might serve, the needs of users, the types of interpretations, and anticipated types of misinterpretations. Any imagery used to describe reports should be based on metaphors that evoke appropriate images for educational data. User-needs analysis is the appropriate forum for determining both product design and effective metaphors for aiding in communication.

RECOMMENDATION 6-1: Appropriate user profiles and needs assessments should be considered as part of the integrated design of district-level and market-basket reports. The integration of usability as part of the overall design process is essential because it considers the information needs of the public.

RECOMMENDATION 6-2: The text, graphs, and tables of reports developed for market-basket or district-level reporting should be subjected to standard usability engineering techniques including appropriate usability testing methodologies. The purpose of such procedures would be to make reports more comprehensible to their readers and more accessible to their target audiences.

7

Implications of District-Level and Market-Basket Reporting

The two reporting practices that are the subject of this study represent more than extensions of current NAEP programs and procedures: they are essentially new programs that would result in new NAEP products. Both reporting methods would present new information that would draw attention from new audiences—audiences that, in the past, may have paid little attention to NAEP results. Implementation of either reporting method would pose challenges for NAEP's existing procedures. District-level reporting would affect sampling procedures. Creation of a short form of NAEP has implications for test construction procedures. Both market-basket and district-level reporting would alter analytic and scoring methodologies as well as the number and types of reports to be prepared. Given these factors, implementation of either reporting practice can be expected to have a significant impact on the internal configuration of the NAEP program. Furthermore, the use of data resulting from these reporting methods by policy makers, state and local departments of education, the press, and the lay public could carry consequences for state and local assessment, curriculum, and instruction.

In this chapter, we address questions about the consequences that the two reporting practices might have, specifically: (1) Would either district-level or market-basket reporting pose any threats to the validity of inferences from national and state NAEP? and (2) What are the implications of district-level and market-basket reporting for other state and local assessment programs? In the first section of this chapter, we explore the likely

101

implications of district-level and market-basket reporting on the NAEP program. In the second section, we discuss the impact of the reporting practices on state and local educational systems.

IMPLICATIONS FOR THE NAEP PROGRAM

NAEP is comprised of many interrelated components that work together to form a complex system. A change to any given piece of this system may have consequences for other pieces of the system. Implementation of either district-level or market-basket reporting would require numerous changes.

First, the type and nature of reported data will influence NAEP's sampling and analytic methodologies. Different sampling procedures would be needed to allow reporting of district-level data. Different analytic procedures would be needed to condition on district characteristics rather than state characteristics.

Second, the types and numbers of reports required will affect the complexity and length of time for production. Under district-level reporting, the number of reports produced could increase significantly. Preparation of market-basket results based on synthetic forms would introduce significant complexity.

Third, the uses made of reported data will affect the relative importance of the assessment in schools and the ways schools and students prepare for the assessment. Such changes suggest the need for additional user support and interpretive guidance. Policy would need to be formulated to guide preparation activities.

Hence, changes cannot be enacted capriciously but must be considered in relation to their potential effects on other pieces of the system. In the text below, we expand on this by exploring some of the effects the proposed reporting practices might have on the validity of inferences drawn from NAEP results as well as on NAEP's procedures, policies, and program costs.

Increasing the Stakes

Traditionally, NAEP has been a low-stakes assessment, since decisions about schools, teachers, and individuals have not been based on test results. The move to reporting data for school districts—either via current NAEP or through the short form—brings the level of reporting much closer to those responsible for instruction. As the level of reporting moves to these smaller units, the assessment stakes will likely become even higher for schools and teachers. Increasing the stakes can have a myriad of effects.

First and foremost, increasing the stakes would require immediate attention to security issues. If high stakes consequences were attached to district-level performance on current NAEP or based on the short form, the likelihood of security breaches would increase. Security breaches could compromise NAEP items as well as the items that make up the short form. In anticipation of increased potential for security breaches, item development would need to be stepped up. Furthermore, with higher stakes, test preparation activities would become more of a concern, since inappropriate test preparation practices could unfairly advantage some districts and could affect the validity and integrity of test results. As suggested by Roeber (1994), NAEP's sponsors would need to lay out appropriate and inappropriate test preparation procedures.

Higher stakes also increases motivation to perform well. Currently, students have little incentive to do well on NAEP beyond their own personal pride and exhortations to honor the state. But if districts were able to obtain results (either as part of current NAEP or via the short form), schools and students might demonstrate greater motivation to perform well on the assessment. Previous research examining the effects of motivation on NAEP performance suggested that changes in motivation may be associated with increased performance (Linn, Koretz, & Baker, 1996). For example, Kiplinger and Linn (1992; 1995/1996) studied changes in performance on NAEP items when a block of NAEP mathematics items was embedded in a state assessment used for state and local school accountability purposes; presumably, schools and students are more motivated to perform well on a test used for accountability purposes. Their studies found a small, but statistically significant, effect, suggesting that students performed better on the NAEP items administered as part of the state assessment than on the same items administered as part of NAEP.

If motivation to do well can affect students' performance, then a number of issues may arise. Performance on NAEP may increase—perhaps not as a result of increased skill levels but as a result of increased motivation to demonstrate skill levels. This can degrade the integrity of NAEP as a monitor of educational progress. For example, under district-level reporting for current NAEP, performance gains could be seen in districts that receive results, thereby improving performance for the state. States that have no districts qualifying to receive results may not realize similar gains. It would be impossible to discern whether performance increases represent real skill-level changes or are only an artifact of changes in motivation.

If plans for the short form were implemented, changes in motivation could further affect the comparability of short-form results to regular NAEP results. Depending on the ways schools and districts decide to use short-form results, motivation to do well may increase. These changes in motivation will interfere with hopes that short-form results would be able to compare with main NAEP.

Interpreting Reported Data

Although these reporting approaches have been suggested as ways of making NAEP reports simpler and more interpretable, they may add complexities that require additional clarification. Below-state reporting may attract new audiences, unfamiliar with the goals, purposes, and limitations of NAEP. Such audiences would require assistance in understanding the meanings and implications of NAEP results. NAEP's sponsors could find themselves faced with providing support materials to new and different users to ensure appropriate interpretations of results.

Use of a percent correct metric for market-basket reporting would require considerable support to prevent misinterpretation, even for experienced users of NAEP results. For instance, during the committee's workshop on market-basket reporting, several speakers cautioned that the percent correct scale proposed for use with the market basket (see Table 6-1) differs from the way the public generally views percent correct scores. A number of speakers commented that people typically regard 70 percent as a passing score; scores around 80 percent as indicating proficiency; and scores of 90 percent and above as advanced. What would members of the general public think when they saw that the average American student scored less than 50 percent on the test? Or, that the proficient student only answered 55 percent of the questions correctly? According to one assessment director, "Most test directors [know enough about NAEP to] understand why this might be, but no teacher, parent, or member of the public would consider 55 percent proficient. They would consider that score as representing 'clueless,' perhaps, and would think even less of the test and the educators that would purport to pass off 55 percent as proficient" (National Research Council, 2000). NAEP's sponsors may find that explaining percent correct scores would require substantial interpretive support to their various audiences.

Demand for School and Individual Results

Availability of the short form would fuel the demand for official individual scores as it is likely that the released short forms will be posted on websites, and audiences will be encouraged to "take the test" and get a score (Colvin, 2000). Because the short form could be administered to all children in a specific grade in a manner closely resembling other testing in schools—testing that results in individual score reports—maintaining the prohibition against individual results will be difficult.

District-level reporting may increase the expectation for school and student level results as well. Instructionally useful information about content areas within a subject—for example, geometry and algebra scores, rather than simply overall mathematics scores—is typically available to districts as part of other testing programs and may also become an expectation for NAEP.

Participation in State or Main NAEP

Participation in NAEP may be affected both positively and negatively by the proposed new reporting practices. Assuming resolution of the many technical and logistical issues related to district-level reporting and that few negative consequences are associated with performance, participation in state or main NAEP may increase. Districts may be willing to invest student and teacher time in return for data they consider useful.

For market-basket reporting via the short form, the impact may be the opposite. If districts are able to receive information more quickly with less testing time, they may opt for the use of the short form in place of participating in state or main NAEP.

Increased Program Costs

Moving to either of the proposed reporting methods would have significant cost implications. Increased item development would be needed—due to the security considerations associated with district-level reporting, the number of items released as part of the market basket, and the items needed to construct short forms. Larger numbers of students would be tested to accommodate reporting district-level results, which could substantially increase test administration costs. Scoring procedures for both reporting practices could also introduce additional complexities, which would increase costs associated with data analyses. Increased numbers of reports would be required, since separate reports would be prepared for each participating district and to provide market-basket results. NAEP's sponsors would need to provide interpretive support to assist users of the new products. Thorough evaluation of the costs associated with the reporting methods is essential. And, if these costs are to be passed on to users (either the state or the district), they need to be known and specified prior to considering districts' and states' interest in either program.

IMPLICATIONS FOR STATE AND LOCAL EDUCATIONAL SYSTEMS

States' and districts' educational systems vary widely, making it impossible to characterize in a simple way the role of assessment or the relationships among assessment, curriculum, and instruction. Traditionally, however, assessment either serves an accountability function or as an integral component of the larger instructional system. Since assessment is one aspect of a system with interrelated parts, changes in assessment systems affect curriculum and instruction, as well as what we know about student learning. Likewise, changes in curriculum or instruction affect assessment.

Instructional systems are often initially developed from expectations for student learning. These expectations are structured by curricula that map essential steps in the development of that learning. Schools implement instructional strategies that enable students to reach the identified curricular milestones and expectations. Assessment occurs at appropriate points in the instructional process to inform decision makers about the status of student learning and to provide information for further instructional planning.

In the ideal, each of these components integrally connects to the other components of the instructional system. However, there are a myriad of factors and influences that can negatively affect the symbiotic relationships among the components. Any resulting disconnect between the components can derail student learning, the reporting of learning progress, or the instructional planning essential to continued learning. To avoid these disruptions, recent educational reforms have focused on the alignment of expectations (often called standards), curriculum, instruction, and assessment.

This idealized system is subject to influences by public policy, public relations, community pressure, and other forces outside of the learning system. These additional forces can produce disconnects among components of the system and can result in inefficiencies that can hamper students' opportunities to attain the desired expectations. Thus, it is important to consider the possible effects of district-level and market-basket reporting on state and local curricula and assessment systems. As with any change, the potential implications for local systems of implementing district-level NAEP or market-basket reporting are many and varied.

For local educational systems, the implications of district-level reporting and market-basket or short-form reporting may parallel those anticipated with the implementation of the state NAEP (see discussion in Chapter 3), as well as include implications specific to district-level instructional systems. The text below discusses the likely effects of the two proposed reporting practices on local curricula and assessments.

Assessment Areas, Content, Schedules, and Methodology

Currently, many state assessments are administered at about the same time of year as national and state NAEP. Schedule conflicts have put many districts in the position of having to choose between NAEP and state or local assessments. When faced with such conflicts, districts have tended to withdraw from NAEP participation in order to accommodate the schedule for mandated state and local assessments. But if NAEP results were reported at the district level, there is likely to be more focus on those results. This could cause districts or states to favor NAEP participation over their local assessment programs. Attempts to ensure that students are not over tested or weary at the time of the NAEP testing could lead to changes in current assessment schedules as well as modification of current assessment systems.

Data from a high visibility national assessment may receive more attention than local assessment results. Generally, local curricula and expectations are closely tied with local and state assessment—but not necessarily with NAEP. Comparisons of performance on the two sets of results may portray different pictures about students' accomplishments, differences that may be primarily attributable to alignment between local assessment and instructional programs. As a result, there might be a push to align instruction more closely with what NAEP tests. Or, current assessment systems might be replaced by the short form, given the desires and pressures for comparisons with national benchmarks. Such changes can potentially disrupt the instructional and learning systems currently in place.

Based on information gathered during the committee-sponsored workshops, it might be expected that local assessments would be influenced by the kinds of items and the format of items that are used on NAEP. Workshop participants commented that states have found the release of NAEP items to be useful in guiding item development for state assessments. For example, the use of performance assessments and constructed response questions in NAEP has led to the inclusion of similarly formatted questions in state instruments. Since the research involved in developing NAEP items is often much more extensive than is possible within state research divisions, states feel quite comfortable using the NAEP design as a model in developing their tests. If district-level reporting were implemented, these changes would also be likely for local assessments. The influence of NAEP formats on local assessments may be more pronounced given the number of items released in connection with the market basket. This could benefit the local systems, but only to the degree that the content to be assessed, the testing purposes, and other important characteristics of the test design would dictate the use of such item types. A significant disconnect within the local system of curriculum, instruction, and assessment could be created if there is insufficient alignment between NAEP and local instructional programs.

Approaches to Reporting Results

District-level NAEP reports might also have an effect on the type of information districts report about their own assessments. To reduce confusion for the public, districts might choose a single form of reporting. Most likely, approaches used for the higher visibility (perceived as the "higher priority") assessment would prevail. Thus, districts may adopt the use of NAEP-like achievement levels, scaled scores that appeared consistent with NAEP results, as well as certain statistical and other processes.

This pattern has been seen in statewide assessments. During the committee's workshops, representatives from state assessment offices commented that NAEP's use of achievement levels to summarize performance has been highly influential.[1] Many states have moved to achievement-level

---

[1] It should also be pointed out that the NAEP achievement levels have been the subject of considerable research and debate. Details can be found in National Research Council (1999b) and Hambleton, Brennan, Brown, Dodd, Forsyth, Mehrens, Nelhaus, Reckase, Rindone, van der Linden, & Zwick (2000).

reporting, and some use the same achievement-level descriptors as NAEP. This emulation of NAEP may increase confusion. For example, some misinterpretation has been associated with the achievement levels. One workshop participant noted that results from a recent NAEP administration revealed that 60 percent of their students performed below the proficient level in reading. State legislators interpreted this finding to mean that their students lacked essential reading skills (an interpretation not necessarily justified by the NAEP results) and advocated for revisions in the state reading instruction and assessment program. Under the amended system, students take an oral reading test in second grade, which allows for early identification and remediation of reading problems. Low-performing students then receive an individualized reading program designed to improve their reading mastery (National Research Council, 1999c). While the ultimate result may have benefited low-performing students, the original interpretation of NAEP results may not have been appropriate.

There are marked disadvantages associated with percent correct reporting. Percent correct scores may appear simple to understand, but they are subject to misinterpretation (See Chapter 4). If NAEP moved to reporting percent correct scores on market-basket sets of items, states and districts might be expected to consider following suit. Attempting to share the credibility of NAEP through applying such reporting approaches to local assessments would undermine the effectiveness and the appropriateness of current approaches to the reporting of results for many local assessments.

These and other approaches used by NAEP might initially appear appropriate for local assessment systems. However, attempts to emulate the national assessment in these areas is fraught with obstacles. NAEP's matrix sampling approach, for example, is not appropriate for producing individual student results. The sophistication and complexity of the processes that underlie NAEP development, scoring, and reporting would likely be inappropriate or unachievable for many local assessments due to various factors. These factors include sample size, expertise, and resources at district levels, as well as fundamental issues related to the comparability of score scales, comparability of achievement levels determined with differing groups on differing content using differing procedures, and other technical issues.

Impact on Curriculum

The use of district-level and market-basket reports may also have an impact on the curricular content taught in schools. With highly visible

NAEP results being reported at the district level, via either full NAEP or through the short form, there would be some pressure for curriculum to become more aligned with those assessment results. By definition, the market-basket concept implies a domain being assessed and reported that is narrower than the entire NAEP framework, and the short form would be an even smaller sample of that domain. The impact on curriculum of reporting at the district level is likely to be significant, due to this narrowed focus. The limited set of items would likely reduce the scope of curricular expectations, especially in the context of strong public scrutiny.

Moreover, the market basket might supplant local standards due to their perceived priority. Because the market basket is smaller, it may appear to some to represent a carefully reasoned set of priorities for learning. And because it was developed nationally, the market basket might appear to represent a more general consensus about what students should know and be able to do than a locally generated set of content and standards.

Linking Local Results to NAEP

There might also be attempts to link local level assessment results to NAEP's district-level results, again for purposes of reducing confusion in interpreting results or for "improving" the comparability between results from differing assessments. Workshop participants observed that an appealing feature of district-level reporting for NAEP would be the presumed ability to compare district assessment results with stable external measures of achievement. There are several problems with attempts to link to NAEP. Earlier reports published by the National Research Council have indicated the problematic nature of attempting or touting such connections (National Research Council, 1999a; National Research Council, 1999d).

CONCLUSIONS AND RECOMMENDATIONS

Many of the concerns expressed in this chapter parallel those expressed when state NAEP was first implemented. Although not all the dire predictions for state NAEP came true, there is considerable concern over the potential uses of district-level and market-basket results. Will district-level results be used to rank order districts within the state or across the country?[2]

---

[2]This presupposes that the sampling design and interest levels result in sufficient numbers of participating districts to produce a "cross-district data compendium" like the cross-state data compendia.

Will districts be punished and rewarded for their performance? Will district-level NAEP results become part of schools' accountability systems? If so, what impact will this have on NAEP? Will NAEP's function as a monitor of change be fundamentally altered by below-state reporting? What effect will the release of market-basket sets of item have on state and local instruction systems? Given the potential for varied effects, the same level of effort on program evaluation would be called for as was implemented in connection with the Trial State Assessment. In addition, support systems will be needed to assist states and districts in appropriate uses and interpretations of the new products and reports.

RECOMMENDATION 7-1. If the decision is made to proceed with district-level reporting, NAEP's sponsors should develop and implement a plan for program evaluation, similar to the research conducted during the initial years of the Trial State Assessment, that would investigate the quality and utility of district-level NAEP data.

RECOMMENDATION 7-2: The potential is high for significant impact on curriculum and/or assessment at the local levels. If either district-level reporting or market-basket reporting, with or without a short form, is planned for implementation, the program sponsors should develop and implement intensive support systems to assist districts and states in appropriate uses and interpretations of any such NAEP results reported.

References

Allen, N.L., Carlson, J.E., & Zelenak, C.A. (1998). *The 1996 NAEP technical report.* Washington, DC: U.S. Department of Education.

Ambach, G.M. (2000). *Assuring strong state, school district and school participation in National Assessment of Educational Progress samples.* Statement before the National Assessment Governing Board, Washington, DC.

American Educational Research Association, American Psychological Association, & National Council on Measurement in Education. (1999). *Standards for educational and psychological testing.* Washington, DC: American Educational Research Association.

Beaton, A.E. (1992). *Methodological issues in reporting NAEP results at district and school levels.* Paper commissioned by the National Assessment Governing Board.

Bennett, K.B., & Flach, J.M. (1992). Graphical display: Implications for divided attention, focused attention, and problem-solving. *Human Factors, 34*(5), 513-533.

Blades, M., & Spencer, C. (1986). The implications of psychological theory and methodology for cognitive cartography. *Cartographica, 23,* 113.

Bock, R.D. (1997). Domain scores: A concept for reporting the National Assessment of Educational Progress results. *Assessment in Transition: Monitoring the Nation's Educational Progress: Background Studies, 81,* 102.

Bock, R.D., Thissen, D., & Zimowski, M.F. (1997). IRT estimation of domain scores. *Journal of Educational Measurement, 37,* 197-211.

Bureau of Labor Statistics. (1999). *Consumer expenditure survey 1996-1997* (Report No. 935). Washington, DC: Author.

Campbell, J.R., Voekl, K.E., & Donahue, P.L. (1997). *NAEP 1996 trends in academic progress: Achievement of U.S. students in science, 1969 to 1996; mathematics, 1973 to 1996; reading, 1971 to 1996; and writing, 1984 to 1996* (NCES Report No. 97-985). Washington, DC: U.S. Department of Education.

Carswell, C.M., & Ramzy, C. (1997). Graphing small data sets: Should we bother? *Behaviour and Information Technology, 16,* 61-71.

Carswell, C.M., Frankenberger, S., & Bernhard, D. (1991). Graphing in depth: Perspectives on the use of three-dimensional graphs to represent lower-dimensional data. *Behaviour and Information Technology, 10*(6), 459-474.

Cieslak, P. (2000). *Milwaukee's experience with district-level NAEP results.* Paper presented at the February workshop of the Committee on NAEP Reporting Practices: Investigating District-Level and Market-Based Reporting, National Research Council, Washington, DC.

Cleveland, W.S. (1985). *The elements of graphing data.* Monterey, CA: Wadsworth.

Cleveland, W.S. (1993). *Visualizing Data.* Summit, NJ: Hobart Press.

Cleveland, W.S., & McGill, R. (1984). Graphical perception: Theory, experimentation, and application to the development of graphic methods. *Journal of the American Statistical Association, 70*, 531-534.

Cleveland, W.S., & McGill, R. (1985). Graphical perception and graphical methods for analyzing scientific data. *Science, 229*, 838-833.

Colvin, R.L. (2000). *NAEP Market-basket reporting: A journalist's perspective.* Paper presented at the February workshop of the Committee on NAEP Reporting Practices: Investigating District-Level and Market-Based Reporting, National Research Council, Washington, DC.

Council of Chief State School Officers. (2000). *Annual survey of state student assessment programs: A summary report, fall 1999.* Washington, DC: Author.

Dent, B.D. (1993). *Cartography: Thematic map design* (3rd ed.). Dubuque, IA: William C. Brown.

DeVito, P.J. (1997). The future of the National Assessment of Educational Progress from the states' perspective. In *Assessment in transition: Monitoring the nation's educational progress.* Stanford, CA: National Academy of Education.

Educational Testing Service. (1997a). *NAEP 1996 mathematics report for Milwaukee Public Schools grade 8: Findings from a special study of the National Assessment of Educational Progress.* Princeton, NJ: Author.

Educational Testing Service. (1997b). *NAEP 1996 science report for Milwaukee Public Schools grade 8: Findings from a special study of the National Assessment of Educational Progress.* Author.

Educational Testing Service. (1998). Prepare for mathematics market basket (Chapter 11) and analyze and report on mathematics market basket booklet (Chapter 18, Task 52). In *NAEP 2000: Application for cooperative agreement for the National Assessment of Educational Progress—Technical application.* Author.

Feldt, L.S., & Brennan, R.L. (1989). Reliability. In R.L. Linn (Ed.), *Educational Measurement* 3rd ed. (pp. 105-146). New York, NY: Macmillan.

Forsyth, R.A. (1991). Do NAEP scales yield valid criterion-referenced interpretations? *Educational Measurement: Issues and Practice, 10*(3), 3-9, 16.

Forsyth, R., Hambleton, R., Linn, R., Mislevy, R., & Yen, W. (1996, July 1). *Design and feasibility team report to the National Assessment Governing Board.*

Gillian, D.J., Wickens, C.D., Hollands, J.G., & Carswell, C.M. (1998). Guidelines for presenting quantitative data in HFES publications. *Human Factors, 40*, 28-41.

Glaser, R., Linn, R., & Bohrnstedt, G. (1997). *Assessment in transition: Monitoring the nation's educational progress.* Stanford, CA: National Academy of Education.

Haertel, E.H. (1991). Reasonable inferences for the trial state NAEP given the current design: Inferences that can and cannot be made. In *Assessing student achievement in the states: Background studies*. Stanford, CA: National Academy of Education.

Hambleton, R.K., Brennan, R.L., Brown, W., Dodd, B., Forsyth, R.A., Mehrens, W.A., Nellhaus, J., Reckase, M., Rindone, D., van der Linden, W.J., & Zwick, R. (2000). A response to "Setting Reasonable and Useful Performance Standards" in the National Academy of Sciences' *Grading the nation's report card. Educational Measurement: Issues and Practice, 19*(2), 5-14.

Hambleton, R.K., & Meara, K. (2000). Newspaper coverage of NAEP results, 1990 to 1999. In National Assessment Governing Board (Ed.), *Student performance standards of the National Assessment of Educational Progress: Affirmation and improvements*. Washington, DC: Editor.

Hambleton, R.K., & Slater, S.C. (1996). *Are NAEP executive summary reports understandable to policymakers and educators?* Paper presented at the annual meeting of the National Council on Measurement in Education, New York.

Haney, W., & Madaus, G.F. (1991). Caution on the future of NAEP: Arguments against using NAEP tests and data reporting below the state level. In *Assessing student achievement in the states: Background studies*. Stanford, CA: National Academy of Education.

Hartka, L., & Stancavage, F. (1994). Perspectives on the impact of the 1994 trial state assessments: State assessment directors, state mathematics specialists, and state reading specialists. In *Quality and utility: The 1994 trial state assessment in reading: Background studies*. Stanford, CA: National Academy of Education.

Herrmann, D., & Pickle, L.W. (1996). A cognitive subtask model of statistical map reading. *Visual Cognition, 3*, 165-190.

Hubel, D.H., & Weisel, T.N. (1965). Receptive fields of single neurons in two nonstiate visual areas (18 and 19) of the cat. *Journal of Neurophysiology, 28*, 229-289.

Hubel, D.H., & Weisel, T.N. (1979). Brain mechanisms and vision. *Scientific American.* 241(3), 150-162.

Jaeger, R.M. (1996). *Reporting large scale assessment results for public consumption: Some propositions and palliatives*. Paper presented at the annual meeting of the National Council on Measurement in Education, New York.

Jaeger, R.M. (1998, September). *Reporting the results of the National Assessment of Educational Progress*. Paper commissioned by the NAEP Validity Studies Panel.

Johnson, E., Lazer, S., & O'Sullivan, C. (1997). *NAEP reconfigured: An integrated redesign of the National Assessment of Educational Progress*. Washington, DC: National Center for Education Statistics.

Kenney, P.A. (2000). *Market basket reporting for NAEP: A content perspective*. Paper presented at the March workshop of the Committee on NAEP Reporting Practices: Investigating District-Level and Market-Based Reporting, National Research Council, Washington, DC.

Kiplinger, V.L., & Linn, R.L. (1992). *Raising the stakes of test administration: The impact on student performance on NAEP* (CSE Technical Report No. 360). Los Angeles, CA: University of California, National Center for Research on Evaluation, Standards, and Student Testing.

Kiplinger, V.L., & Linn, R.L. (1995/1996). Raising the stakes of test administration: The impact of student performance on NAEP. *Educational Assessment, 3*, 311-333.

Kolen, M.J., & Brennan, R.L. (1995). *Test equating methods and practices.* New York, NY: Springer-Verlag.

Kolstad, A. (2000). *Simplifying the interpretation of NAEP results with market baskets and shortened forms of NAEP.* Paper presented at the February workshop of the Committee on NAEP Reporting Practices: Investigating District-Level and Market-Based Reporting, National Research Council, Washington, DC.

Koretz, D.M. (1991). State comparisons using NAEP: Large costs, disappointing benefits. *Educational Researcher, 20*(3), 19-21.

Koretz, D.M., & Deibert, E. (1995/1996). Setting standards and interpreting achievement: A cautionary tale from the National Assessment of Educational Progress. *Educational Assessment, 3*(1), 53-81.

Kosslyn S. (1985). Graphics and human information processing. *Journal of the American Statistical Association, 80*, 499-512.

Kosslyn, S. (1994). *Elements of graph design.* New York, NY: W. H. Freeman.

Linn, R.L., Koretz, D., & Baker, E.L. (1996). *Assessing the validity of the National Assessment of Educational Progress: NAEP technical review panel white paper.* Los Angeles, CA: University of California, National Center for Research on Evaluation, Standards, and Student Testing.

Lord, F.M., & Novick, M.R. (1968). *Statistical theories of mental test scores.* Reading, MA: Addison-Wesley.

Mazzeo, J. (2000). *NAEP's year-2000 market-basket study: What do we expect to learn?* Paper presented at the February workshop of the Committee on NAEP Reporting Practices: Investigating District-Level and Market-Based Reporting, National Research Council, Washington, DC.

McConachie, M. (2000). *State policy perspectives on NAEP market basket reporting.* Paper presented at the February workshop of the Committee on NAEP Reporting Practices: Investigating District-Level and Market-Based Reporting, National Research Council, Washington, DC.

McDonald, R.P. (1999). *Test theory: A unified approach.* Mahwah, NJ: Lawrence Erlbaum.

McDonnell, L.M. (1994). *Policymakers' views of student assessment.* Report commissioned by the Office of Educational Research and Improvement, U.S. Department of Education. Santa Monica, CA: RAND Institute on Education and Training.

Milroy, R., & Poulton, E.C. (1978). Labeling graphs for increased reading speed. *Ergonomics, 22*, 55-61.

Mislevy, R. (2000). *Evidentiary relationships among data-gathering methods and reporting scales in surveys of educational achievement.* Paper presented at the February workshop of the Committee on NAEP Reporting Practices: Investigating District-Level and Market-Based Reporting, National Research Council, Washington, DC.

Monmonier, M. (1991). *How to lie with maps.* Chicago, IL: University of Chicago Press.

National Assessment Governing Board. (1995a). *Guidelines for the conduct of below-state NAEP assessments, draft implementation document.* Washington, DC: Author.

National Assessment Governing Board. (1995b). *Guidelines for the conduct of below-state NAEP assessments, policy statement.* Washington, DC: Author.

National Assessment Governing Board. (1996). *Redesigning the National Assessment of Education Progress, policy statement.* Washington, DC: Author.

National Assessment Governing Board. (1997). *Resolution on market basket reporting, report of August 2.* Washington, DC: Author.

National Assessment Governing Board. (1999a). *The National Assessment of Educational Progress: Design 2000-2010.* Washington, DC: Author.

National Assessment Governing Board. (1999b, November). *Policy guidance on the NAEP short form.* Washington, DC: Author.

National Assessment Governing Board. (1999c). *Reporting and Dissemination Committee agenda of November 19.* Washington, DC: Author.

National Assessment Governing Board. (1999d). *Reporting and Dissemination Committee report of August 6.* Washington, DC: Author.

National Assessment Governing Board. (2000a). *Design and Methodology Committee agenda of August 4.* Washington, DC: Author.

National Assessment Governing Board. (2000b). *Mathematics framework for the 1996 and 2000 National Assessment of Educational Progress.* [On-line]. Available http://www.nagb.org.

National Center for Education Statistics. (1995). *Draft guidelines and technical specifications for the conduct of below-state NAEP assessments.* Washington, DC: Author.

National Center for Education Statistics. (2000a, May 9). *A brief history of NAEP participation.* Paper prepared for meeting of the Design and Analysis Committee, Washington, DC: Author.

National Center for Education Statistics. (2000b, May 9). *Rewards for NAEP: Proposals and consequences.* Paper prepared for meeting of the Design and Analysis Committee, Washington, DC: Author.

National Research Council. (1999a). *Embedding questions: The pursuit of a common measure in uncommon tests.* Committee on Embedding Common Test Items in State and District Assessments. D.M. Koretz, M.W. Bertenthal, & B.F. Green, (Eds.), Board on Testing and Assessment, Commission on Behavioral and Social Sciences and Education. Washington, DC: National Academy Press.

National Research Council. (1999b). *Grading the nation's report card: Evaluating NAEP and transforming the assessment of educational progress.* Committee on Evaluation of National and State Assessments of Educational Progress. J.W. Pellegrino, L.R. Jones, & K.M. Mitchell, (Eds.), Commission on Behavioral and Social Sciences and Education. Washington, DC: National Academy Press.

National Research Council. (1999c). *Reporting district-level NAEP data: Summary of a workshop.* Committee on NAEP Reporting Practices: Investigating District-Level and Market-Basket Reporting. P.J. DeVito & J.A. Koenig, (Eds.), Board on Testing and Assessment, Commission on Behavioral and Social Sciences and Education. Washington, DC: National Academy Press.

National Research Council. (1999d). *Uncommon measures: Equivalence and linkage among educational tests.* Committee on Equivalency and Linkage of Educational Tests. M.J. Feuer, P.W. Holland, B.F. Green, M.W. Bertenthal, & F.C. Hemphill, (Eds.), Commission on Behavioral and Social Sciences and Education. Washington, DC: National Academy Press.

National Research Council. (2000). *Designing a market-basket for NAEP: Summary of a workshop.* Committee on NAEP Reporting Practices: Investigating District-Level and Market-Basket Reporting. P.J. DeVito & J.A. Koenig, (Eds.), Board on Testing and Assessment. Washington, DC: National Academy Press.

Neilsen, J. (1993). *Usability engineering.* San Diego, CA: Morgan Kaufmann.

Norman, D.A. (1988). *The psychology of everyday things.* New York, NY: Basic Books.

Nunnally, J.C. (1967). *Psychometric theory.* New York, NY: McGraw-Hill.

O'Reilly, J. (2000). *District level and market-basket reporting: A district perspective.* Paper presented at the February workshop of the Committee on NAEP Reporting Practices: Investigating District-Level and Market-Based Reporting, National Research Council, Washington, DC.

Pickle, L.W., & Herrmann, D. (1994). The process of reading statistical maps: The effect of color. *Statistical Computing and Statistical Graphics Newsletter, 5*(1), 1,12-16.

Pommerich, M., & Nicewander, W.A. (1998). *Estimating average domain scores.* Iowa City, IA: American College Testing.

Roeber, E.D. (1994). *Guidelines for the use of NAEP at the district and school levels.* Paper commissioned by the National Assessment Governing Board. February.

Rubin, D.B. (1987). *Multiple imputation for nonresponse in surveys.* New York, NY: John Wiley & Sons.

Rubin, J. (1994). *Handbook of usability testing.* New York, NY: John Wiley & Sons.

Rust, K. (1999). *NAEP sample designs and district level reporting.* Paper prepared for the National Research Council Workshop on District-Level Reporting, Washington, DC.

Selden, R. (1991). The case for district- and school-level results from NAEP. In *Assessing student achievement in the states: Background studies.* Stanford, CA: National Academy of Education.

Simkin, D., & Hastie, R. (1987). An information processing analysis of graph perception. *Journal of the American Statistical Association, 82,* 454-465.

Spence, I., & Lewandowski, S. (1989). Robust multidimensional scaling. *Psychometrika, 54*(3).

Stancavage, F.B., Roeber, E., & Bohrnstedt, G.H. (1992). A study of the impact of reporting the results of the 1990 trial state assessment: First report. *Assessing student achievement in the states: Background studies.* Stanford, CA: National Academy of Education.

Stancavage, F.B., Roeber, E., & Bohrnstedt, G.H. (1993). Impact of the 1990 trial state assessment: A follow up study. *The trial state assessment: Prospects and realities: Background studies.* Stanford, CA: National Academy of Education.

Stanley, J.C. (1971). Reliability. In R.L. Thorndike (Ed.), *Educational measurement* (2nd ed.). Washington, DC: American Council on Education.

Truby, R. (2000, February). *A market basket for NAEP: Policies and objectives of the National Assessment Governing Board.* Paper presented at the workshop of the Committee on NAEP Reporting Practices: Investigating District-Level and Market-Based Reporting, National Research Council, Washington, DC.

Tversky, B., & Schiano, D.J. (1989). Perceptual and conceptual factors in distortions in memory for graphs and maps. *Journal of Experimental Psychology: General, 118*(4), 387-398.

U.S. Department of Education. National Center for Education Statistics. (1999). Horkay, N. (Ed.), *The NAEP guide* (NCES Report No. 2000-456).

Vernon, M.D. (1952). The use and value of graphical methods of presenting quantitative data. *Occupational Psychology, 26,* 22-24.

Wainer, H. (1997a). Improving tabular displays with NAEP tables as examples and inspirations. *Journal of Educational and Behavioral Statistics, 22,* 1-30.

Wainer, H. (1997b). *Visual revelations: Graphical tales of fate and deception from Napoleon Bonaparte to Ross Perot.* New York: Copernicus.

Wainer, H., Hambleton, R.K., & Meara, K. (1999). Alternative displays for communicating NAEP results: A redesign and validity study. *Journal of Educational Measurement, 36*(4), 301-335.

Williams, P.L., Reese, C.M., Campbell, J.R., Mazzeo, J., & Phillips, G.W. (1995). *NAEP 1994 reading: A first look.* Washington, DC: United States Department of Education.

Background and Current Uses of the Consumer Price Index

The CPI is a measure of the average change over time in the prices paid by urban consumers in the United States for a fixed basket of goods in a fixed geographic area. The CPI was developed during World War I so that the federal government could establish cost-of-living adjustments for workers in shipbuilding centers. Rapid increases in prices had made such an index necessary for calculating these adjustments.

Today, the CPI is the principal source of information concerning trends in consumer prices and inflation in the United States. It is widely used as an economic indicator and a means of adjusting other economic series (e.g., retail sales, hourly earnings) and dollar values used in government programs. The CPI is used to adjust payments to Social Security recipients and to Federal and military retirees, and for a number of entitlement programs such as food stamps and school lunches. Also, individual income tax brackets and personal exemptions are adjusted for inflation using the CPI. The index's impact on the finances of the federal government is significant. In fiscal year 1996, for example, the Office of Management and Budget estimated that each one-percent increase in the CPI produced a $5.7 billion increase in outlays and a $2.5 billion decline in revenues. In addition, as the most widely used index for measuring inflation, the CPI aids in the formulation of fiscal and monetary policies and in economic decision-making.

The CPI measures the rates of changes in prices, not their absolute levels. Most of the specific CPI indexes have a 1982-84 reference base.

That is, the average price level for the 36-month period covering these years is established as having an index level of 100. A 10-percent increase in price since this reference period would then correspond to an index level of 110.

The Bureau of Labor Statistics currently produces two national indices every month: the CPI for All Urban Consumers (CPI-U) and the more narrowly based CPI for Urban Wage Earners and Clerical Workers (CPI-W), which is developed using only data from households represented in certain occupations. In addition to monthly release of the national CPI estimates, the BLS publishes monthly indexes for the four principal regions of the nation (Northeast, Midwest, South, and West), as well as for collective urban areas classified by population size. The BLS also publishes indexes for 26 local areas on monthly, bimonthly, or semiannual schedules. An individual area index measures how much prices have changed over a specific time interval in that particular area. However, because of the nature of the index and the specifics of the sampling design, indexes cannot be used for relative comparisons of the level of prices or the cost of living in different geographic areas. In fact, the compositions of the regional market baskets generally vary substantially across areas because of differences in purchasing patterns.

COLLECTION OF DATA ON CONSUMER EXPENDITURES

The BLS develops the CPI market basket on the basis of detailed information provided by families and individuals about their actual purchases. Information on purchases is gathered from households in the Consumer Expenditure (CE) Survey, which consists of two components: an interview survey and a diary survey.[1] Each component has its own questionnaire and sample.

In the quarterly interview portion of the CE survey, an interviewer visits every consumer in the sample every 3 months over a 12-month period. The CE interview survey is designed to collect data on the types of expenditures that respondents can be expected to recall for a period of 3 months or longer. These expenditures include major purchases, such as

---

[1]Much of the material in this section is excerpted from Appendix B of *Consumer Expenditure Survey, 1996-97*, Report 935, Bureau of Labor Statistics, September 1999.

property, automobiles, and major appliances, and expenses that occur on a regular basis, such as rent, insurance premiums, and utilities. Expenditures incurred on trips are also reported in this survey. The CE interview survey thus collects detailed data on 60 to 70 percent of total household expenditures. Global estimates—i.e., expense patterns for a 3-month period—are obtained for food and other selected items, accounting for an additional 20 percent to 25 percent of total household expenditures.

In the diary component of the CE survey, consumers are asked to maintain a complete record of expenses for two consecutive one-week periods. The CE diary survey was designed to obtain detailed data on frequently purchased small items, including food and beverages (both at home and in eating places), tobacco, housekeeping supplies, nonprescription drugs, and personal care products and services. Respondents are less likely to recall such items over long periods. Integrating data from the interview and diary surveys thus provides a complete accounting of expenditures and income.

Both the interview and diary surveys collect data on household characteristics and income. Data on household characteristics are used to determine the eligibility of the family for inclusion in the population covered by the Consumer Price Index, to classify families for purposes of analysis, and to adjust for nonresponse by families who do not complete the survey. Household demographic characteristics are also used to integrate data from the interview and diary components.

Samples for both the interview and diary components of the Consumer Expenditure Survey are national probability samples of households designed to be representative of the total U.S. civilian population. Sampling occurs in two stages. The first stage of sampling involves the selection of primary sampling units (PSUs) that consist of counties, groups of counties, and portions of counties. The PSUs are classified into four categories: (1) large metropolitan statistical areas (MSAs); (2) medium-sized MSAs; (3) nonmetropolitan areas that are included in the CPI; and (4) nonmetropolitan areas where only the urban population is included in the CPI. Lists of housing units in each PSU are constructed using decennial census data and supplemental information on new housing construction. The second stage of sampling involves the selection of housing units from each PSU for participation in the CE survey.

The interview component is a panel rotation survey. Each panel, a set of selected addresses, is interviewed for five consecutive quarters and then dropped from the survey. As one panel leaves the survey, a new panel is introduced. Thus, approximately 20 percent of the addresses are new to the survey each month. For the 1996 and 1997 CE interview surveys, approximately 9,000 addresses were selected in each quarter. Allowing for nonresponses, the number of suitable interviews per quarter was targeted at approximately 5,400. Thus, more than 5,000 families participate in the interview survey in any given calendar year.

The diary component involves drawing a new sample each year, independent both of previous years and of the sample for the interview component. Approximately 7,000 addresses were contacted for the 1996 and 1997 CE diary surveys. Allowing for nonresponses, the number of households providing usable diaries was targeted at approximately 5,400 per year.

CONSTRUCTION OF THE CPI MARKET-BASKET SYSTEM

The BLS prices the CPI market basket and produces the monthly CPI index using a complex, multistage sampling process. The first stage involves the selection of urban areas that will constitute the CPI geographic sample. Because the CPI market basket is constructed using data from the CE survey, the geographic areas selected for the CPI-U are also used in the CE survey. Once selected, the CPI geographic sample is fixed for 10 years until new census data become available. Using the information supplied by families in the CE surveys, the BLS constructs the CPI market basket by partitioning the set of all consumer goods and services into a hierarchy of increasingly detailed categories, referred to as the CPI item structure.[2] The levels of the CPI classification are:

- All items
- Major groups
- Intermediate aggregates
- Expenditure classes
- Item strata (or categories)
- Entry level items

For example, in developing the current market basket the BLS has classified expenditures reported in the 1993-95 CE survey into more than

---

[2] Much of the material in this section and the next section is excerpted from CPI materials available at the Bureau of Labor Statistics web site, http://www.bls.gov.

200 item strata arranged into eight major groups: food and beverages; housing; apparel; transportation; medical care; recreation; education and communication; and other goods and services. For each geographic area (primary sampling unit) included in the CPI geographic sample, the BLS assigns each item category an expenditure weight, or importance, based on its share of total family expenditures. Aggregating weights from the geographic areas in the CPI sample derives item category weights at the national level. Thus, one can ultimately view the CPI market basket as a set of item strata and associated expenditure weights.

MONTHLY DATA COLLECTION AND PRICING

Following the sampling process, BLS analysts select the outlets (places where area residents make purchases), goods and services (specific items purchased), and residents' housing units to be used in computing the monthly CPI. Selection of the CPI outlet and item samples is based on information from the Telephone Point-of-Purchase Survey (TPOPS), a household survey that provides BLS with a sampling frame of outlets and retail establishments visited by urban consumers. The TPOPS obtains data from about 17,000 families annually on the types of goods and services consumers purchase, the amount of these expenditures, and the places the expenditures are made. Since the 1998 CPI revision, TPOPS data have been collected using computer-assisted telephone interviews (CATI), which allows a portion of all commodities and services to be updated, or rotated, in each sampling unit every year.

Within item categories, BLS statisticians select hundreds of entry-level items and match them with the sampled retail outlets for price collection. The number of price quotations and observations to be obtained is determined statistically with the objective of producing the most accurate national all-items index as possible, subject to available funds. The BLS field staff who collect CPI prices use the entry-level items as the starting point for the selection of the unique products or services—within the outlet— whose prices will be monitored. This selection is made using a random probability sampling method that reflects an item's relative share of sales at that particular store.

Each month, BLS data collectors, called economic assistants, visit or call thousands of retail stores, service establishments, rental units, and doctors' offices throughout the United States to obtain price information on the thousands of items used to track and measure price change in the CPI.

These economic assistants record the prices of about 80,000 items each month. These 80,000 prices thus represent a scientifically selected sample of the prices paid by consumers for goods and services purchased.

UPDATING AND IMPROVING THE CPI MARKET BASKET

Because of the many important uses of the monthly CPI, there is great interest in insuring that the CPI market basket accurately reflects changes in consumption over time. Each decade, data from the U.S. census of population and housing are used to update the CPI process in three key respects: (1) redesigning the national geographic sample to reflect shifts in population; (2) revising the CPI item structure to represent current consumption patterns; and (3) modifying the expenditure weights to reflect changes in the item structure as well as reallocation of the family budget.

In response to growing demands for a more current CPI market basket, the BLS has redesigned some of the survey processes to enable more frequent revision than once every five or ten years. In particular, the new TPOPS sample design permits a shift to sample rotation by category rather than by geographic area, thereby facilitating accelerated sample rotation in product areas where the markets are most dynamic. The sample rotation involves (1) reselecting the retail stores and business establishments to be visited by BLS field representatives and (2) reselecting the unique products and services to be priced for the market basket. For example, to represent the market basket item category "records and tapes," a cassette tape sold in Outlet A could be replaced by a compact disc sold in Outlet B. In addition, the sample size of the ongoing CE survey has been increased substantially, which will enable the production of updated expenditure weights every two years starting in January 2002.

B

Depicting Changes in Reading Scores— An Example of a Usability Evaluation

To illustrate how the usability evaluation might work, we will focus on the redesign of a single data display from the report *NAEP 1994 Reading: A First Look Report* (Williams, Reese, Campbell, Mazzeo, & Phillips, 1995). This report is designed for a broad audience of policy makers, educators, and the press. Wainer and colleagues (1997a, 1999) redesigned several displays from the report in accord with specific usability standards described in *Visual Revelations* (Wainer, 1997b). These revisions were evaluated through formal usability trials in which preference and comprehension measures were taken (Wainer et al., 1999). We discuss the design modifications that resulted in one of Wainer's more successful redesigns and then illustrate how the processes shown in Box 6-1 (see Chapter 6) might be applied to make the illustration still more usable and accessible.

The original display appears in Figure B-1 and shows test scores as a function of administration date (1992 and 1994), grade (fourth, eighth, or twelfth), and geographic region (Central, Northeast, Southeast, and West). The format chosen is a perspective-view bar graph with region represented along the horizontal axis and grade represented in depth (z-axis). Scores for both years are shown, side by side, for each grade within each region. Numerical data values are placed above the tops of the individual bars. In his revision, Wainer selected a two-dimensional line-graph for these data, and he removed the raw numerical values from the display. Year of administration was represented on the horizontal axis and all other conditions were labeled by line grouping (grade) or by individual line (region) directly

FIGURE B-1 Wainer, H.; Hambleton, R.K., and Meara, K. (1999). Alternative displays for communicating NAEP results: a redesign and validity study. *Journal of Educational Measurement*, 36(4), 301-335. Copyright 1999 by the National Council on Measurement in Education; reproduced with permission from the publisher.

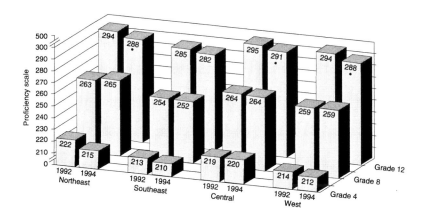

*Significant decrease between 1992 and 1994.

by the relevant display objects. He also included a legend to help readers identify individual lines. The revision appears in Figure B-2.

WHAT WOULD WE LEARN FROM A USER NEEDS ANALYSIS?

Before beginning to revise the display again, it is essential to have a list of user requirements based on the results of user-needs analysis. This would involve bringing together small "user panels" comprised of people representing the range of individuals who may be exposed to NAEP data reports. Note that the emphasis here is on *diversity* rather than *typicality* of potential group members. Thus, parents with limited educational backgrounds should be included as well as educators who may have extensive backgrounds in educational testing. Policy makers with very different political agendas should be chosen, as well as members of the local and national press.

Once user panels are established, then focus groups, semi-structured brainstorming sessions, individual interviews, and other related methods

FIGURE B-2 Wainer, H.; Hambleton, R.K., and Meara, K. (1999). Alternative displays for communicating NAEP results: a redesign and validity study. *Journal of Educational Measurement*, 36(4), 301-335. Copyright 1999 by the National Council on Measurement in Education; reproduced with permission from the publisher.

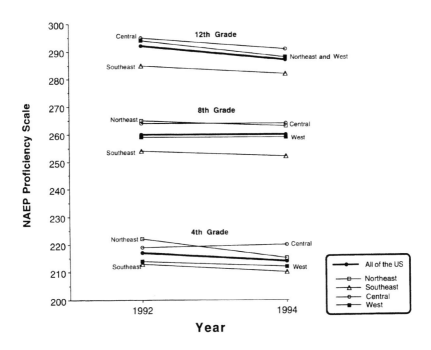

can be held to determine the expectations of group members. One of the most important questions in redesigning an existing display, is what the users would like to know. What kinds of conclusions would they like to be able to draw? By giving panelists the data sets in a number of formats (numerical data tables and existing graphs in the present case), it would be possible to see which interpretations are spontaneously made, as well as the order in which these conclusions are drawn. Since the data presentation format will influence the nature of these spontaneous interpretations (Carswell and Ramzy, 1997), it is important to consider the conclusions drawn from the various formats. Alternatively, the data parameters could be verbally described to them and panelists allowed the chance to ask questions. For instance, they could be told:

We have average NAEP reading test scores from 1992 and 1994. These are reported separately for the 2nd, 8th, and 12th grades. Data are also broken down by region—western, central, southeastern, or northeastern schools. What would you like to know about these data?

Tracking panelists' questions is an effective method for eliciting the informational needs of potential users.

To illustrate, suppose that these methods revealed that the following questions were asked of the 1992-1994 change data in the following order:

(1) Were we (the United States as a whole) doing better or worse in 1994?

(2) Which regions were showing the most change and in which direction?

(3) What kind of change occurred in my region?

(4) How does the change that occurred in my region compare to that found in other regions?

These questions should drive decisions about the content and structure of data displays. In addition, when performing usability tests on the comprehensibility of the data display, users' abilities to answer these questions accurately should be a core criterion of design success. With the information needs of the users better understood, one or more usability analysts can perform a heuristic evaluation.

HEURISTIC EVALUATION
OF THE ORIGINAL AND REVISED DISPLAYS

In the text that follows, we evaluate the original and revised displays (Figures B-1 and B-2) of the 1992 and 1994 NAEP reading data by applying the heuristics proposed for the review of NAEP reports (Box 6-1). In addition, we propose changes to be made in the next design iteration.

Is the format compatible with the performance criterion selected?

Suppose that the questions raised during a hypothetical user-needs analysis revealed that users were primarily interested in ordinal information (e.g., "Did scores increase or decrease from 1992 to 1994?" "Did region X's scores increase/decrease more than region Y's?"). It is likely that the readers would want quick access to this information. Thus, a graphical display, rather than a table, is the appropriate choice. This also suggests that displaying the exact data values in conjunction with the graph, as in the original bar chart, may be unnecessary and may even impede rapid access of the comparative information. Our revised display, like the two previous versions, will be graphical. And, as with the previously revised display, we will not report numeric values.

Is the structure of the display compatible with the structure of the data?

This heuristic is probably not relevant in the present case. Besides test scores, two (theoretically) continuous variables are displayed in the present data set–grade level and year of test administration. However, the present data describe only three grade levels and two test years. Thus, we can say very little about the relationship between either of the latter two variables and test scores.

Is the perceptual grouping of information compatible with the mental grouping users must perform to extract the information they want and need?

The findings from our hypothetical user-needs analysis suggest that users clearly want to make comparisons and that they are most interested in comparing scores across test administration years. Thus, the two years for each of the region-grade combinations must be tightly grouped so that they can be perceived together. In the original graphic (Figure B-1), the two years were presented side by side, allowing grouping by proximity. In the revised graph (Figure B-2), the two data points were not close together relative to other data points, such as those showing test means for other regions; however, the two administrations for each region-grade condition were connected by a line. In the next revision of the graph, the 1992 and 1994 values should be connected by line segments, but they should also be closer than in the first revision.

A second issue is the relative tightness of the grouping of data pairs for 1992 and 1994 values across the same region versus across the same grade level. That is, should all of the data for a *region* be grouped together or should all of the data for a *single grade* be grouped together? In the original graph (Figure B-1), the data for a given year appeared in the same horizontal row perpendicular to the line of sight, while the data for a given region fell along a row parallel to the line of sight. Thus, grouping by region and grouping by grade are about equally strong. The first revision (Figure B-2) made grouping by grade stronger through spatial proximity, which allows easier access to comparisons among different regions within a grade level. Because our hypothetical user-need analysis suggested that comparisons among regions were of greater importance, we would propose continuing to group by grade level so that data from different regions appear side by side. We would further highlight regional comparisons by adding a regional boundary around (or "frame") the data from each grade level.

Is the level of numeric detail compatible with the reliability of the data and the needs of the reader?

Based on our hypothetical findings, we would drop the numeric means from the graph, as in the first revision (Figure B-2). Given the users' interest in the mean score changes from 1992 to 1994, reliability becomes important; that is, are the differences between the two mean scores reliable? Perhaps pairs of scores (i.e., pairs of bars in the original graph and line segments in the revised graph) could be coded as exceeding or not exceeding a specific reliability criterion. For example, in the original figure, pairs that were significantly different were coded with asterisks on one of the two bars.

Is data salience compatible with data importance?

As described above, statistically reliable changes in scores across test administrations should be differentiated from those that are not reliable. The asterisk used in the original figure (Figure B-1) is not highly attention getting. Color could be used for this purpose and, possibly, a more saturated color could highlight the reliable differences.

In terms of the relative salience of other graphic elements, the revised graph clearly highlights changes in scores from 1992 to 1994 that are different in magnitude or direction across the geographic regions. However, this salience may actually be misleading in making certain perceptual comparisons across grade levels. On the other hand, the original graph does not clearly highlight unusual changes in scores. Its placement of individual data points on the page tends to call attention to fourth-grade scores because they appear closer to the reader than the other scores in this "3-d" graph. This organization would be warranted if based on the perception that the audience is most interested in the fourth-grade scores. Otherwise, this organization could be a misuse of salience cues. In the revised graph (Figure B-2), lengths of the lines connecting scores from the same grade-region will draw attention to the largest changes from 1992 to 1994.

Is the data display compatible with working memory limits?

One crude way of evaluating if a data display is compatible with working memory limits is to simply count the number of groups of elements, as well as the number of elements in each of these groups. For example, the original graph (Figure B-1) could be described as 12 pairs of bars, or 12 groups of two elements. The revised graph (Figure B-2) could be described as three groups of five lines. A closer look should be taken whenever the number of major groups, or number of elements within those groups, is greater than four. Thus, the "12 pairs" and "five lines" of the original and revised graphs, respectively, could pose some difficulties for working memory, depending on the tasks to be performed. If a reader is simply trying to count the number of times test scores appeared to decrease across the years, then exceeding the "rule of fours" is probably not a big problem. However, it might be different if an individual were trying to capture all instances of decreasing scores to generate causal hypotheses. One sugges-tion for the redesign of the original graph (Figure B-1) would be to create more distinctive groups for different grade levels. This would lead to three groups of four pairs of bars, which may help readers "chunk" information in working memory in a more manageable way.

In the initial revision of the graph of reading scores (Figure B-2), two problems are evident. First, as noted, there are five lines in each of the three grade-level groupings. In addition to scores from the four regions, a fifth line represents mean scores across the entire United States. This would seem to be important data to represent directly, given our hypothetical users' need to know how students in the United States are performing across the two years. However, it may not be necessary to know the mean value of test scores during both years to answer this question. Simply determining the overall pattern of the graphic—whether the lines seem to be mostly "going up" or "going down"—may suffice. Therefore, we would suggest removing the line showing the national means.

A second problem relates to the use of legends to identify regions on the revised graph (a number of lines per group problem). Different point symbols are used for each of the four regions, and the overall United States data are represented by a different line-style and point-symbol combination. Memorizing five symbols can be difficult; a problem that can often be remedied by placing labels directly by the lines in a graph (Milroy & Poulton, 1978). An attempt was made to do this in the revised graph; nevertheless, because the lines overlap, the user must still rely on the symbols described in the legend. Again, dropping one of the lines would help the overlap problem that prevents use of the labels to the side of the lines. In addition, it would reduce the load on working memory by ensuring that readers are more likely to correctly identify the different lines, even when it is necessary to refer to the legend.

Are physical properties of the stimuli compatible with our ability to detect, discriminate, and recognize these properties?

Both the original graph and the revised graph use differences in position along an aligned scale to represent differences in performance between 1992 and 1994 for each region-grade combination. According to work by Cleveland and McGill (1984, 1985), this is one of the most accurate perceptual comparisons that can be made. Comparisons across different regions and grades within a given year are also made by comparing points along a common scale in the revised figure (Figure B-2). In the original figure, comparisons across grades are based on differences in position of bar heights along nonaligned common scales. People are less accurate at these judgments. In the revised figure, comparisons of changes across region-grade conditions are to be made by comparing line slopes. Generally, people do not make accurate estimates of relative slopes. For a new revision of the graph, we would recommend devising a format that uses line lengths, which are more likely to be correctly interpreted.

We should also be aware of the potential visual distortions or illusions that can occur in both the original and revised graphs. In the original graph, the use of linear perspective and other depth cues (e.g., occlusion) can lead to size illusions, with the size of the bars in the front of the graph underestimated relative to the ones in the back. With line graphs, designers should be aware that we often judge slope relative to nearby frameworks such as other lines. The revised graph (Figure B-2) demonstrates this type of illusion. For example, the central region appears to have a very large increase in fourth graders' performance across the two-year testing interval. This change is actually only one-fourth the size of the decrease in scores among twelfth graders for the same region. However, the line graph seems to show that the increase among fourth graders is at least as big as the decrease among twelfth graders. The reason for this misperception is that the slope of a line tends to be over or under estimated depending on the slopes of surrounding lines (and particularly lines that intersect the target line). Specifically, for the fourth-grade data, the positively sloping line for the central region intersects with a negatively sloping line for the northeast region. This presentation tends to accentuate the slope of each. This is known as the Poggendorf illusion (Hubel & Wiesel, 1965, 1979). We will attempt to avoid the use of both perspective and line slope in our revision of the NAEP reading scores graph.

Is the organization of information in the display compatible with spatial metaphors and population stereotypes?

When the purpose is to show regional differences, the display should consider cartographic conventions of representing North at the top of a map and West to the far left. A display that must order information about geographic regions across a page should conform to the left-for-West rule. In our case, this means that the following left-to-right arrangement of regions should be used: West, Central, Southeast, and Northeast. Neither the original or revised graphs use this ordering. In the original graph (Figure B-1), the map convention is reversed, with the most eastern region on the left of the page. In the revised graph (Figure B-2), the regions are ordered according to their mean scores.

Is the choice of display format and ornamentation compatible with the users' preferences and biases?

There is evidence that people are more likely to distrust data presented in perspective (3-D) displays (Carswell, Frankenberger, and Bernhard, 1991), such as the original graph. Further, evidence suggests that people less familiar with graphs tend to feel less threatened by bar graphs than by line graphs (Vernon, 1952). In our revision of the graph, we will avoid the use of perspective and the use of traditional line graphs as well.

THE REVISED GRAPH

Based on the changes suggested by the heuristic evaluation described above, we produced the graph shown in Figure B-3. Note that position on common aligned scales is maintained for comparisons of scores across administrations and across regions within a grade level. However, absolute-score comparisons across grade levels cannot be made with this format. Since the hypothetical user-needs analysis indicated that few users would try to make such comparisons, we felt justified in sacrificing this piece of information. In return, the revised graph enables the use of length judgments for comparing the magnitude of changes among different regions and grades.

The data are grouped into three clearly demarcated panels by grade level. Within each grade level there are four lines, each representing the two mean scores for a region. Rather than connecting two points that are offset horizontally, the revised graph uses two points along the same vertical grid line to represent the two test administration dates. The end of the line representing the second administration is indicated by an arrowhead. For each grade level, the four regions are arranged from left to right using the West-to-East map convention.

In addition, several other changes will simplify the presentation. The term "Midwest" was substituted for the term "Central" in order to streamline the axis labels. The grade-level panels were offset from left to right to mimic the spatial metaphor of moving through the grades as if climbing a staircase. Footnotes and legends were deleted. Instead, a few explanatory comments were presented as part of the graph's title where they are more likely to be read.

A USABILITY TEST:
IS THE NEW GRAPH BETTER THAN THE EARLIER VERSIONS?

Even though we have a redesigned graph that incorporates findings from the user-needs analysis and the heuristic evaluation, we still would not know if the new design were actually better or preferred by users. Accordingly, the next step must be usability testing similar to that described by Wainer and colleagues (1999). The multiple versions of the graph should be viewed by different groups of subjects representative of the intended audiences. Users should be asked what they learned from the graph, and researchers should note whether or not users drew conclusions relevant to the major questions defined in the user needs analysis. These interpretations can be timed, and follow-up questions can be asked to determine if users can access important information. Preference data should also be

FIGURE B-3 Changes in Regional NAEP Reading Scores from 1992 to 1994. The direction and length of arrows indicate the direction and size of the change in average scores. A diamond indicates that the average score remaind the same.

Grade 12

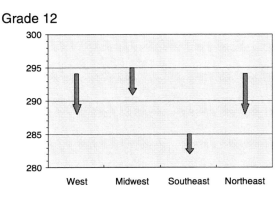

Grade 8

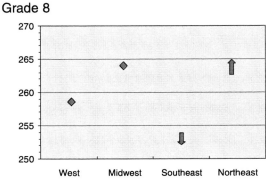

Grade 4

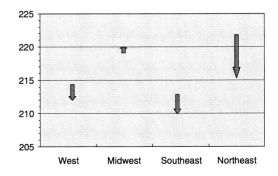

collected after allowing participating users to view all three versions of the graphs. There are many variations of usability tests, and many additional methods are described in Rubin (1994) and Neilsen (1993).

If the graph were to be included in the next release of NAEP reports, then data on citations, requests for publication, and misinterpretations by the press can also be collected to gauge display comprehensibility and accessibility. These data should guide future revisions.

Biographical Data

Pasquale DeVito (*Chair*) is the former director of the Office of Assessment and Information Services for the Rhode Island Department of Education. He was recently named the Director of the Board on Testing and Assessment. His research and expertise include educational research, measurement, and evaluation and related policy making. Dr. DeVito has a Ph.D. in educational research, measurement, and evaluation from Boston College.

Linda Rochelle Bryant is principal of Westwood Elementary School in Pittsburgh, Pennsylvania. She is a former science teacher of elementary and middle school students and has served as a member of the National Assessment Governing Board and as chair of the math/science committee of the National Assessment of Educational Progress. She received a B.A. in elementary education from the University of South Carolina and an M.A. in elementary education from the University of Pittsburgh.

Catherine Melody Carswell is an associate professor of psychology at the University of Kentucky. Her principal research interests are the effects of interface design on performance in human-machine and user-product systems. Dr. Carswell has published extensively on subjects such as graph comprehension, the perceptual organization of visual displays, and the effects of personal preference on display usability. She received her Ph.D. from the University of Illinois, Urbana-Champaign.

Maryellen Donahue is director of Research, Assessment, and Evaluation for the Boston Public Schools. She has published and presented on various aspects of assessment including its role in accountability, quality standards, and implementation issues in performance assessment. She obtained a B.A. in English and Sociology from Maryville University, a M.A. in reading from the University of Massachusetts, and has completed doctoral work in educational measurement at Boston College.

Louis M. Fabrizio is director of the Division of Accountability Services of the North Carolina Department of Public Instruction. He has previously worked as assessment and evaluation consultant to CTB/McGraw-Hill, Head Start director, and mathematics and science teacher. He serves as a member of the Technical Advisory Committee for the Voluntary National Test and the assessment subcommittee for the Education Information Advisory Committee. He received a B.S in physics from Georgetown University and a M.S. in education administration and supervision from North Carolina State University.

LeAnn M. Gamache is director of Assessment and Evaluation for Littleton Public Schools in Littleton, Colorado. Previously, Dr. Gamache served as the Director of Psychometric Services at ACT. She has published and presented on several aspects of assessment including statistical comparison of test items, gender differentiated prediction, and the role of testing in training. Dr. Gamache received her Ph.D. in educational measurement and statistics from the University of Iowa.

Douglas J. Herrmann is chair of the Department of Psychology at Indiana State University. He was the founding director of the Collection Procedures Research Laboratory at the U.S. Bureau of Labor Statistics, and has served as senior cognitive psychologist at the National Center for Health Statistics. He has written and edited several textbooks on the psychology of memory. He received a Ph.D. in experimental psychology from the University of Delaware.

Kaeli Knowles is a program officer with the Board on Testing and Assessment at the National Academy of Sciences/National Research Council. Concurrent with her work on the Committee on the National Assessment of Educational Progress Reporting Practices, she works with the Committee on Assessment and Teacher Quality. Prior to joining BOTA, she was employed as a guidance counselor for five years. She has a B.A. in psychology from the University of Richmond, a M.Ed. in counseling from the University of Virginia, and a Ph.D. in educational psychology from the University of Maryland.

Judith Anderson Koenig (*Study Director*) is a program officer with the Board on Testing and Assessment at the National Academy of Sciences/National Research Council. Previously, she worked for the Association of American Medical Colleges where she was a senior research associate for the Medical College Admission Test program. She has a B.A. in special education from Michigan State University, a M.A. in psychology from George Mason University, and is enrolled in a doctoral program in measurement, statistics, and evaluation at the University of Maryland, College Park.

Karen J. Mitchell is a senior program officer with the Board on Testing and Assessment at the National Academy of Sciences/National Research Council. Previously, she was at RAND, where she conducted research on student assessment, education reform, and education policy. She has a B.A. in early childhood and elementary education from Wesleyan College and M.S. and Ph.D. degrees, both in educational research methodology, from Cornell University.

Audrey Qualls is an associate professor of educational measurement and statistics at the University of Iowa. Her research and expertise include development of large-scale achievement assessments and indicators of early learning, score reliability, and appropriate uses of standardized test information. Dr. Qualls has a Ph.D. in educational measurement and statistics from the University of Iowa. She previously served as a member of the NRC Committee on Appropriate Test Use.

Mark Daniel Reckase is a professor of measurement and quantitative methods in the Department of Counseling, Educational Psychology and Special Education at Michigan State University. His research focuses on modeling of the interaction of persons and test items; multidimensional models of the persons item interactions; and computer applications to measurement of cognitive skills. He has numerous publications on innovative assessment approaches, item response theory, performance assessment, and computer applications to testing. He received a Ph.D. in psychology from Syracuse University.

Duane L. Steffey is an associate professor of mathematical and computer sciences at San Diego State University. Previously, he served as a study director with the Committee on National Statistics with the National Academy of Sciences/National Research Council. He has published on statistical methods, particularly on hierarchical Bayesian modeling, and has engaged broadly in interdisciplinary research and consulting. He received a Ph.D. in statistics from Carnegie Mellon University.